THIS

BELONGS

TO

ROBERT

ATKINS

HIDDEN TREASURES

NORTH OXFORDSHIRE

Edited by Claire Tupholme

First published in Great Britain in 2002 by
YOUNG WRITERS
Remus House,
Coltsfoot Drive,
Peterborough, PE2 9JX
Telephone (01733) 890066

HB ISBN 0 75434 030 9
SB ISBN 0 75434 031 7

FOREWORD

This year, the Young Writers' Hidden Treasures competition proudly presents a showcase of the best poetic talent from over 72,000 up-and-coming writers nationwide.

Young Writers was established in 1991 and we are still successful, even in today's technologically-led world, in promoting and encouraging the reading and writing of poetry.

The thought, effort, imagination and hard work put into each poem impressed us all, and once again, the task of selecting poems was a difficult one, but nevertheless, an enjoyable experience.

We hope you are as pleased as we are with the final selection and that you and your family continue to be entertained with *Hidden Treasures North Oxfordshire* for many years to come.

CONTENTS

James Gwyn	70
Wade Tallis	70
Robert McGregor	70
Matthew Sherwood	71
Jasmin Whiteford	71
Joshua Keith	71
Bethany Hewitt	72
Lauren Stanford	72
Jessica Tuffrey	73
Michael	74

Kings Meadow Primary School

Matthew Crook	74
Sophie Yazdi	75
Zoe Gordon	75
Heather Luckhurst	76
Aaron Jell	76
Dipesh Mistry	77
Danielle Howard	78
Chloe Anne Straiton	78
Katie Brown	79
Rebecca Train	79
Daniel Crook	80
Gemma Sweetman	80
Connie Hollyer	81
Jessica Scott	81
Thomas Smith	82
Laura Burchell	82
Ellie Seddon	83
Lewis Gordon	83
Melissa Hawkes-Blackburn	84
Charlie Sutcliffe	84
Maddison Butler	84
Robyn Cook	85
Sophie Bebb	85
Andrew Green	85
Chloe Davis	86
Aimee Cross	86

Robert Howkins	87
Rebecca Cross	87
Carianne Rudge	88
Rachel Cullup-Smith	88
Stephanie Clapp	89
Adam Edmonds	90
Lauren Clough	90
Alice Wise	90
Jessica Martin	91
Shannon Walker	91
Sarah Willacy	92
Craig Whitty	92
Michael Brindle	93
Ben Hopkins Hill	93
Jordan Wilson	94
Laura Clarke	94
Louise Slade	94

Middle Barton Primary School

Laura Howe	95
Gemma Jackman	95
Lewis Fowler	96
Marni Banks	96

Newbottle & Charlton CE Primary School

Timothy Clapham	97
Clare Hawes	97
Nick Swallow	98
Jonathan Stevens	98
Emma Blake	98
Sophie Jones	99
Bethany Talbot	99
Nial Hoggarth	99
Caitlin Joss	100
Tom Brown	100
Emma Davidson	100
Ryan Knight	101
Angelina Marsella Brookes	101

The Poems

YUM! I LOVE THAT STUFF!

Hot, brown, fried bacon,
Sizzling in a pan.

Yum, I love that stuff!

Cool, mouth-watering chocolate,
Melting in my mouth.

Yum, I love that stuff!

New vanilla ice cream,
Waiting in the fridge.

Yum, I love that stuff!

Delicious roast turkey,
Waiting on my plate . . .

Yum, I love them *all!*

Rebecca Harper (9)
Bishop Loveday CE Primary School

LIFE

L   ive a life so happy,
I   s a life so long?
V   alue your life forever,
E   lse all around will go wrong.

L   ive a life so miserable,
I   s a life so short?
V   alue your life forever,
E   very bit of your life is caught.

Verity Smette (10)
Bishop Loveday CE Primary School

HOMEWORK

Homework is a nightmare,
That never, ever ends,
It gives me such a headache
And sends me round the bend!

From the very first time school started,
I had English, science and maths,
So in doing my horrible homework,
I had to prepare for my nerve-wracking SATs!

The worst thing about all of this is,
The teachers just smile and say,
'Just do your best and take your time,
But I want it in by Friday.'

I do take good care of my homework,
I like ripping it into bits
And I do promise my teachers I'll do it,
But end up listening to CD hits!

Genna Macmillan (10)
Bishop Loveday CE Primary School

TABBY CATS

Two tabby cats playing
Each in their own way
Soft and gentle they play
Special every day.

Abigail Harper (9)
Bishop Loveday CE Primary School

THE MAGIC BOWL

I was down at the dump exploring,
A regular habit of mine.
There seemed nothing there of interest
Until something odd caught my eye.

I rummaged around, it turned out to be
A clay bowl all chipped and cracked.
I eased it out of a heap of tins
Inside which it was tightly packed.

I was strangely attracted to it
And I somehow knew what to do.
I picked it up and stared at it blankly:
'Show me the ghost ship's ghostly crew!'

There they were, translucent and pallid,
In the bowl - yet still in their ship.
'Show me slave-masters of long ago!'
They were right there, lashing their whips.

I knelt down in front of my saviour,
My ticket to freedom and joy.
The world came to me there in that dump
From Chinese girl to Negro boy.

Completely the best thing in the world
Or so it seemed to me - but
Soon it had taken hold of my soul.
I had been fooled so easily.

I wasted away at that idol,
My heart was enslaved in a wink.
Beware - all that glistens is not gold!
Before you let go, stop and think.

Imogen Phillips (9)
Bishop Loveday CE Primary School

HIDDEN TREASURES

Little people looking for tombs
Which have lost treasures inside them
Booby traps are inside them too
So be careful with them
You might set them off!
So do what the book shows,
Look for the money
And for the treasures too.
If you let them off you will not come back!
If you do make it back with the hidden treasures,
You will be rich!
So we will think you will make it,
So try to make it,
Because your family is missing you.
It might have some diamonds in the hidden treasures,
Or might not.
You will never know,
Only if you go there to find out.
So go there
And you will find out yourself.

Joshua Hawkes (10)
Chipping Warden Primary School

HIDDEN TREASURES

Clever, clever me
I was sat in a tree
But then came along
Sammy and then
I fell out of the tree
Suddenly a magpie
Took my 10p
So me and Sammy
Went after the magpie

And then Sammy fell over me
He dropped his 50p
And the magpie took it
So then we were angry
So we chased after the magpie
Then the magpie
Dropped our money
Because he hit a tree
And fell on me
And gave me
The back door key.

Dale Fradd (11)
Chipping Warden Primary School

HIDDEN TREASURE

Mansions are creepy,
Old and screechy.
Make you all be scared,
But if you know,
You could just go,
To get the treasure in there.
It could be old.
Spiders unfold,
The gold and silver too.
Golden cups, silver mugs
And bronze plates too.
I want the gold,
To be rich until I'm old,
So I can buy nice things too.
Go to the house,
Creep like a mouse
Or the monster
Will eat you!

Harry Davies (9)
Chipping Warden Primary School

HIDDEN TREASURE

I'm trying to find an Egyptian tomb,
There may be booby traps
And loud booms!
Egyptian hieroglyphics are everywhere
And all my men are very scared.
I ask a man to pass me
A hammer and a chisel.
As I hit a massive crack,
Scarabs appear and get
Nearer and nearer
As we jump over the scarabs.
The tomb has caught my eye,
As we arrive over the pit,
I have to pass a record of challenges.
As I jump the
Spinning blade and monkey bar,
The lava pit,
I reach the final challenge,
As I duck the swinging axe,
I finally reach the tomb.

Sam Fradd (9)
Chipping Warden Primary School

HIDDEN TREASURES

A diver dives to the bottom of the sea,
To find hidden treasures for me.
He came back up with a very loud cough,
But all he could find was an old moth.
He went back down with a frown
And when he came up he had found an old crown.
So he went back down deep, deep, deep,
As we watched the dolphins leap.
He came back up with a broken hand,
While he was down there, it got stuck in the sand.

Down again into the reeds,
Up again with a packet of seeds.
What hidden treasures would be found?
Given up its secrets, would the sea mind?
So at the end I've found my treasure,
Hasn't it been a real pleasure?
Home I go, hip hip hooray!
I had a brilliant day!

Ashley Turner (10)
Chipping Warden Primary School

HIDDEN TREASURE

Under the sea
Deep, deep down
Clever machines
Digging under the sand
Dig, dig, dig
What will we find?
Hopefully gold
One hour, two hours
Time ticks by
When will we find it?
Hopefully soon
Suddenly a bang
What was that?
A big, heavy chest
With a sunken ship too
The chest flies open
The gold jumps out
Just what we wanted
So up to the top into the boat
And out with the stash.

David Jobbins (10)
Chipping Warden Primary School

HIDDEN TREASURES

My necklace has been lost,
Don't know how much it cost.
Not yet found,
Searched underground and all around.

Searching in the sand,
With the sun so grand.
I don't know where to look,
I don't think it is under my book.
After all, I'd had a look.

It is gold with a locket
And I keep it in my pocket.
It has a picture of my mum and dad,
I'm sure they won't be very glad.

Not yet found so I will look in my house,
It is too big for a mouse.
I shall think of where I last had it,
I hope this won't be a habit.

I will look in my room,
Quick get a broom!
I will think in my head,
Oh yes, it is under my *bed!*

Roseanne Davies (11)
Chipping Warden Primary School

HIDDEN TREASURE

Under the sea
In the sand
A treasure lays
People have tried to recover it
But all have failed
Now people think it is impossible
But now a man has hope
He dreams
Gold, silver and jewels
He tries hard
And one day he will find
The one thing he wants
He dived
With high hopes
He looks
Then realises
A compass
Pointing at the wall
He smashes the wall
And there is the treasure
In his glory
He takes it back
With a smile
He becomes a superstar
The man who found the treasure.

James Buck (10)
Chipping Warden Primary School

HIDDEN TREASURES

Where is it?
I have looked everywhere
I don't know where to find it
I've looked here and there
The thing I am looking for
Can't have got far
It's not like it has legs
And it can't have driven away in a car
I am trying to remember
Where I had it last
But I still can't find it
It got lost so fast
I've got so tired
I've been looking round
So I think I'll have a rest
A little sit down
Suddenly I remember
I had it yesterday
I put it on my bed
In a funny sort of way
I'm going up to my bed
Up the stairs I go
I wonder if it's still there
We'll have to see, I don't know
It was on my bed
Where I thought to look
I'm so glad I've got it
My nice, old book!

Holly Nash (9)
Chipping Warden Primary School

Hidden Treasure

Digging up, turning over,
Thick soil getting wetter,
Lots of creepy-crawlies here,
With every dig we're getting better.

What's this? It's something hard,
Maybe it is brick or stone
Or is it some sort of treasure?
I know! It's a pot in the shape of a cone.

It's the middle of the day; it's getting hot,
Oh great, here is another find!
All our finds in shady spots,
It's a pot full of mouldy bacon rind!

At the end of the day the plan went fine
And now we're packing up,
But tomorrow holds more great things,
Spoons and forks, plates and cups.

Oh what a beautiful sunrise,
I wonder what awaits us today?
Because we're very excited,
It's the final piece of the golden plate, *hooray!*

Now the excavation's finished,
We're driving to the museum,
We're very happy with our finds,
We hope other people like them too!

James Clarke (11)
Chipping Warden Primary School

HIDDEN TREASURE

Where is all the hidden treasure
In the treasure hunt today?
What will you find? What will we find?
Come on, let's go and play!

Have you looked everywhere?
There surely must be some here,
Under leaves, behind stones,
Into scary places, but there's no fear!

Let's look over here and there,
Maybe it's behind this tree,
Come on everybody now,
You'll never know what we'll see!

What have you found?
Nothing yet,
Only some clothes on the washing line,
Hang on, what's in that net?

A precious stone and more,
A bracelet and a diamond ring,
An emerald necklace, pure stones,
What a pretty thing.

Hey, what's our dog doing?
He's digging up the plant.
Now he's got something in his mouth,
He can't, he can't.

Now he's coming up here,
Maybe it's a cone,
But wait, no it's not,
It's a dirty, smelly bone!

Olivia Clarke (9)
Chipping Warden Primary School

HIDDEN TREASURE

Looking for my treasure
Where could it be?
My map says in some water
That must mean the sea
I'll have to hire a submarine
In colours red and green

I'll have to buy a scuba suit
And with matching boots
I'm still hunting for my treasure
I hope I'll find it soon
By the time I get there
It will be a full moon

I'm in my submarine
I'm moving in between
Lots of big, grey rocks
I hope all the doors are locked

I'm at my destination
Deep down in the sea
I hope it is down here
Where else could it be?

I've nearly found my treasure
And now I can see
A white gleaming pearl
Meant just for me!

Charlotte Davies (9)
Chipping Warden Primary School

HIDDEN TREASURE

At the beach,
On the sand,
Digging a hole,
Really deep,
Got bored,
Got a boat,
Sailed away on the sea.
Rocked all the way,
Finally got to shore,
Walked away,
Looked around,
Saw some food,
Ate it straight away.
Sat on a thorn,
Jumped on my feet,
Said, 'I'm going to dig for treasure!'
Got a spade,
Digging away,
Hit something hard.
Dug some more
And saw a door,
Opened it up and went straight in,
Looked around and saw a man.
I went *aahh!*
Got some necklaces and ran away.
Got on the boat
And rode away.
Got back home, said, 'Look at this!'
Went back in my room,
Said, 'Yahoo!'

Jonathan Pearson (10)
Chipping Warden Primary School

HIDDEN TREASURE

I'm covered in mould and seaweed,
My hidden treasure you won't find,
For none are left behind.

My crew are no longer here,
Lying underneath the sea,
The water took them far and near,
My treasure of gold and silver,
Your doom is drawing near.

The storm began,
I could not see
Anywhere in front of me,
I thought I might die,
As waves washed over me.

I saw a wreck
And jumped on deck,
I saw some gold
Amongst the mould.

I swam to the surface,
Gasping for air,
'I've found it,' I cried,
The gold is mine.

I saw a shark,
A moment later, I was in its jaws,
Swimming on all fours.

Harriet Woodford (11)
Chipping Warden Primary School

HIDDEN TREASURE

If you look under the sea,
You never know what treasure you'll see.
Maybe there's treasure underground?
If there is, it should be found.
Maybe there's treasures in a pot,
If there is, I'll get the lot.

If there's treasures up in space,
I'll be there in a race.
If there's treasure in the beachy land,
I'll be there digging up the sand.
If there's treasure somewhere in Spain,
I'll be in a hurry to catch the plane.

If there's treasure that can float,
I'll be there in a boat.
If there's treasure anywhere around,
I'll be there making a sound.
If there's treasure anywhere,
I'll not be sitting in my chair.

Jonathan Charter (9)
Chipping Warden Primary School

HIDDEN TREASURE

Digging, digging
Long ago
What will they find?
Who knows!
Digging, digging
Underground
When they find something
Will they laugh?
Will they cry?

Digging, digging
Will there be a curse?
Well, who knows!
Have thieves been?
Everyone's thoughts!
Digging, digging
A metal sound
Have they hit something?
Is it the dreaded curse?
No, it's some lovely
Shiny gold!

Georgina Rumble (10)
Chipping Warden Primary School

HIDDEN TREASURES

Some people think that the best hidden treasures are,
Dazzling diamonds, gleaming gold, perfect pearls
That they find under the sea or under the ground,
But the wisest people know that the best hidden treasures are
Talent, love, to care for people and animals,
These treasures shine brighter than day,
You can't find these under the sea
Or under the ground,
You have to look inside,
Everyone has one,
They cost nothing at all,
It costs nothing to use,
It's wonderful to see them shining so brilliantly bright,
Shine, shine, shine!

Hannah Theobald (10)
Culworth Endowed CE Primary School

A HIDDEN TREASURE

A hidden treasure is fun.
A hidden treasure is happiness.
A hidden treasure is hope.
A hidden treasure is a tear.
A hidden treasure is love.
A hidden treasure is world peace.

Thomas Garrood (10)
Culworth Endowed CE Primary School

LOVE

Love is the deepest red,
As red as the blood of innocent wounds.
It lives in the heart of deepest passion.
It smells like the sweetest flowers on Earth,
All put together into a big bouquet.
It feels like the most beautiful, softest silk,
Sent from a land far, faraway.
It tastes like the sweetest sugar.
Love sounds like the morning chorus of all the birds on Earth.

Anna Tasker (9)
Culworth Endowed CE Primary School

MY NANNA

My nanna is the greatest,
She rocks, she rolls, she hip hops and dives,
She is a whizz with all the crosswords,
As happy as a flock of birds!

She might have a few little wrinkles,
Her shopping skills are just a *bang!*
So come rain or shine,
She's making good time,
So worry not, 'cause age is fine!

Charlotte-Saskia Payne-Clarke (9)
Culworth Endowed CE Primary School

THE MAGIC BOX

I will put in my box . . .
Chinese chopsticks changing colour,
Traffic lights showing bronze, silver, gold,
Slithery, slimy snakes eating salt sausages.

I will put in the box . . .
A flower singing in the summer sun,
A breath of air from the autumn breeze,
The door moaning when it shuts.

I will put in the box . . .
Five whispers spoken in Trati,
The last wave from an ancient aunty,
The first word from a baby.

I will put in my box . . .
18 months of golden sky,
The fire puts out freezing water.
My box is decorated with fresh fruits,
With a layer of chocolate.
I shall skate in my box,
On sparkling blue ice,
On the seas of Russia.

Joe Mumford, Sam Rollason & Scott Gardener (10)
Deddington CE Primary School

POLAR BEAR

As the cold north winds blow,
The polar bear emerges from the snow.
Its glossy coat swaying in the moonlight
And it's running with all its might.
The Arctic Ocean is its goal,
Searching for fish swimming in shoals.
He slowly dives into the ice-cold sea,
Swimming round playfully.
Quickly dodging shoals of fish,
Granted by his every wish.
It's slowly creeping towards the end of the day,
There's no more time to swim or play.

Katie Lay (10)
Deddington CE Primary School

CHINESE FIREBALL

Chinese fireball
Is not very cool.
Chinese fireball
Is so very hot.
Chinese fireball,
Hotter than a pot.

Chinese fireball
Isn't a foul
And if you ever meet
Just run!
If you don't, it won't be neat.

Devon Horne (10)
Deddington CE Primary School

THE MAGIC BOX

I will put in the box
Frogs that are fine for Friday saying ribbit ribbit

The smoke of a bomb
That has just been lit, bang, bang, bang

I will put in the box
Six sizzling sausages
Singing silly sizzle, sizzle, sizzle

I will put in the box
A dog walking a human,
Children teaching, teachers learning

My box is fashioned from silver and gold,
With crystals, diamonds and rubies
With six sausages, frogs, smoke and a log.

Louise Cowley (10)
Deddington CE Primary School

HORIZON

The horizon goes down at night,
The sky goes blue and white.
The moon comes out,
The stars peep through,
Then the birds start to fly through.
As morning draws in,
The sun comes up,
But we all still know,
The moon's still out.

Arriane Munson (10)
Deddington CE Primary School

THE PLAYGROUND

The rusty, old gate screeches as you enter the playground,
Shoes chatter as they run outside,
Cars cough as they park outside,
Conkers sing a war song as they go into battle,
Balls cheer as loud as they can when they fly into the net,
Skipping ropes dance and sing as children jump,
Knees wail and roar as they hit the ground,
Hoops roly-poly and somersault laughing as they go,
The window cries out for help as it gets shattered by the ball.

Luc Thornton & Sam Rollason (11)
Deddington CE Primary School

INSIDE THE CHURCH!

Inside the church,
Rusty, old, gloomy pictures chatter,
Moonlight roars against the stained glass windows,
The old, battered doors open and close with a scream,
Candles cry and cry when they are alight,
The organ sings with a laughter and a grin.

Natalie Rowles (10)
Deddington CE Primary School

THE BOX

I open the box to the sweet smell of roses.
I open the box to the wind that streams through my hair.
I open the box to a warm summer's day.
I open the box to the sound of children laughing and playing.
I open the box full of *surprises!*

Rosie Best (11)
Deddington CE Primary School

THE MAGIC BOX!

I will put in my box . . .
A wave of a ball gown under the sparkling stars,
A pinch of sand from the Egyptian deserts,
A tip of a finger touching a tiger's tooth.

I will put in my box . . .
The window that stood and giggled
As it sang the song of the sea's crashing waves,
The whale of the ocean,
Sounds of the sea,
The cycle of life that will ride forever.

I will put in my box . . .
The dark red wishes of the silver seas,
The wave of an ending friendship,
The first cry of a newborn infant.

I will put in my box . . .
The book that read the human,
The paper that inked the pen,
13 months and a deep purple sun.

My box is designed from fresh-water pearls
And sparkling icicles with stars on the top
And a shining moon on the bottom,
The hinges are ruby-red bangles.

I shall swim in my box on the high water waves,
Then float ashore on the smooth, golden sand,
The colour of sparkling treasure!

Laura Mawby (10)
Deddington CE Primary School

THE LONELY CASTLE

There once was a castle in a forest so green,
It was as tall as the trees and stood by a stream.
It shone in the sun and glowed in the snow
And who lived there? Nobody knows.

For hundreds of years it stood on this ground,
It once was alive with magical sounds
Of princes and wizards, maidens and knights,
Who all set the forest shining alight.

Amongst howling wolves and whistling winds,
Hooting owls and ghost-like things,
It now stands alone, empty and bare . . .
No one ever dares go there!

Nancy Hall (10)
Deddington CE Primary School

KITCHEN CLANG!

The clanking of the saucepans,
The singing of the kettle,
The chirping of the teacups,
The kitchen will not settle!
The giggling of the tea bags,
The dancing of the spoons,
The jumping of the dinner plates,
The tap is playing tunes!
So if you're in the kitchen at night,
I can guarantee, you're in for a fright!

Anna McGovern (11)
Deddington CE Primary School

NIGHTMARE WOOD

This is a poem about a little girl
Who lived in a town so far, far away,
One night she could not find her cat,
So she went to find her cat.
She was nowhere to be found,
So she went to Nightmare Wood
And saw things you can only dream about.

There were dark elves and goblins to werewolves and ogres,
But the little girl carried on walking
Because she wanted her cat,
She walked for hours, never stopping.

Next day the town was in shock,
The little princess was not in her bed
And how do I know this?
Because I've seen things you can only dream of!

Matthew Hunsley (10)
Deddington CE Primary School

THONY, THE CAT

Thony, the cat wiped his paws on the doormat,
When he had just come home from out in the cold.
He went to his mat and sat down for a while,
When he heard the tap.
The little brown cat went over to the tap
To see that the water dripping into a very big hat.
The fat brown cat went back over to his mat
And had a very long catnap.

Kate Alsworth (10)
Deddington CE Primary School

THE CASTLE

There once was a castle
But now there's only a site
I wonder what could have happened there?
There might have been a fight.

Did the castle have a moat,
A drawbridge, turrets, even a king?
Was it defended by knights
And did its jesters often sing?

I wonder how it disappeared?
It might have fallen into ruin
Or did people knock it down
Because it was too difficult for renewing?

I'd like to live in a castle,
But it might be very lonely.
So I'd invite my friends around
And that would make it homely.

Jack Davies (10)
Deddington CE Primary School

CHILDREN!

When the children go to bed,
Better watch out,
They might bump their head.
Children in different countries,
White, black or brown,
Might come in their sleepy dressing gown.
Snuggled up tight, *boo!*
Don't get a fright.

Nicole Lewis (11)
Deddington CE Primary School

MY LITTLE BROTHER IS A PAIN

My little brother puts spiders in my bed,
Once he locked me in the shed.
He plays tricks on me day and night,
When I just go to sleep he wakes me up by turning on the light.
He puts water balloons on my chair,
He sprays colouring in my hair.
My little brother turns his music on full blast,
He gobbles up his food really fast.

But he is my brother after all,
But don't tell him I like him at all.

Sam Rollason (11)
Deddington CE Primary School

A LIFE OF A HIPPO

As a hippo sleeps through the day
His mother said to go and play
Chasing other hippos
This is the life
Sitting down all day and night

A life of a hippo, playing all day
And this is where I like to stay
Swimming underwater is so much fun

Have a tasty meal before we go
Staying with my mum and dad
Playing in the mud
Before we go to sleep.

Gillian Ross (11)
Deddington CE Primary School

THE ENCHANTED WORLD

The enchanted world is full of yummy things,
Flying things, things such as trees with sweets on,
Chocolate apples and grapes with gooey caramel inside,
Flying dogs with chocolate tails
And horses with sweets that hang down from their manes,
Flying pigs made of marshmallow,
There are scooters that fly when you go on them
And bouncy boats that send you up high into the sky,
But all I know that is one day,
I am going to the enchanted world to see what it is really like.

Holly Spengler (9)
Deddington CE Primary School

THE SUN AND ITS SHADOW

The sun shone bright
But not at night
The shadow glared at the floor
The kids all played in delight
Then when the sun went down
The moon came out
Until the morning was found
The sun smiled at the kids in delight
Then the sun said a little rhyme
The ruler says, 'How are you?'
The moon says, 'Fine.'
The stars say, 'Enjoy the peace.'
The sun says, 'I will!'

Hannah Corner (10)
Deddington CE Primary School

POINT-TO-POINT

The horses are walking round the ring just thinking
Soon they will be pounding their hearts out to get past the post
The jockeys are coming out the weighing room
Now the secretary rings the bell
And all the jockeys can mount on their horses
And then the huntsmen blows the horn
And the jockeys follow him out
They go and see if they are able to jump the fences
Then they trot to the starting
The commentator says they are on the starter's orders and they're off
First a jockey tumbles but they both are all right
They are coming to the last jump before home
They jump it clear
One horse called First Winner pounds in front
And is a length away from the others
And he does it, he wins the Grand National
Then the horse falls and he is winded
From pounding his heart out
But his jockey is proud of him
The trainer has to come to take him home.

Victoria Humphries (10)
Deddington CE Primary School

EGYPTIAN LAUNDRY WOMAN

I can hear my friends washing clothes in the river, singing
I can smell the delicious mouth-watering bread baking,
I can taste the juicy grapes,
I can feel the sun on my skin,
I see the pyramids in the distance,
They look like triangles of gold.

Paige Kaye (7)
Deddington CE Primary School

MY TEACHER

My teacher is a real bore,
She makes us snore and snore.
My favourite subject is history,
Because she makes it a real mystery.
When we hear the home time bell,
We really, really yell.
I want to play in the sun,
Now it's home time, *run!*

Isobella Radini (10)
Deddington CE Primary School

QUEEN

The Queen is special,
She is cool,
I saw her once out of school,
She is very pretty
With her lovely crown on,
The Queen is
Cool!

Natasha Large (10)
Deddington CE Primary School

THE BULLY

As I stand here
The names they call
They make me cry
I try to ignore
But the more they call
The more I cry.

Ben Powell (8)
Deddington CE Primary School

WAITING FOR SPRING

The hills and fields are covered in white,
Then all of a sudden the waiting is over,
Trees are growing taller while the leaves are sprouting,
Flowers open their little eyelids and peep out,
As if they are shouting,
'Spring is here once more.'

Danielle Pritchard (8)
Deddington CE Primary School

LITTLE ELF

One day a little elf fell onto my hand
It thought I was an enemy and pulled out a rubber band
It flung the band and it hit me on the nose
I fell and the little elf thought I was doing a pose.

Nicole Whitehead (9)
Deddington CE Primary School

DARK EYES

His eyes were blue,
As blue as the crashing waves in the harbour,
As blue as gleaming sapphires in the earth.
As white as the frothy sea,
As white as running milk.
As black as the darkest feelings,
As black as the Devil's mind.

Patrick Campbell (9)
Deddington CE Primary School

IN THE TOMB

In the tomb
I smell the smoke of my fire lamp.
I taste the crusty spiderweb!
I see a glint of gold coming ever so closer in my mind.
I hear the soft creak of a brick move nearby.
I touch the salty sand on the brick walls.
Huh, what was that? I feel a space in the wall.
This time I really do see
The real glint of gold I was so hoping for.
I charge through the wall that turned out to be a door.
I keep on running, I trip.
I fall head-first into gold, silver, rubies, diamonds, crystals,
I am swimming in them.

Benjamin Teare (8)
Deddington CE Primary School

OUTSIDE THE TOMB

I can smell the lovely smell
Of my mum cooking the meal.
I can taste the horrible bread,
All gritty, sandy and pebbly in my mouth.
I can see the hard walls of the pyramid
Getting taller and taller.
I can hear the shouting and wheels of carts
On the cobbly street.
I can feel the hard tomb wall
Rub gently against my hand.

Jane Allcock (8)
Deddington CE Primary School

THE TOMB

I can see the mummy lying there, waiting,
It is lying there staring.
I can hear my footsteps in the yard,
It's making its way past -
I can feel the cat alive,
It is miaowing at me.
I can smell old, dirty, disgusting bones,
Lying around.
I can feel the sun shining on me,
It feels like my face is burnt.
I taste the spiderweb crawling in my mouth.

Benjamin Lewis (8)
Deddington CE Primary School

MY DAY AT THE THEME PARK

When I got to the theme park
I went mad,
Then I saw the most biggest ride ever,
It was the belly wobble ride.
Your tummy moves sideways
And sometimes people are sick.
It'll try not to.
When I got on it the man pressed on,
I went slow at first then I got faster and faster,
I could see my tummy wobble,
Then I went green and I was *sick!*

Florence Spencer (10)
Deddington CE Primary School

MY DAY AT THE FARM

The other day I went to the farm,
For my friend's party.
Everybody was playing in the park,
I didn't want to play in the park,
So I decided to go and look at the animals on my own,
It all started when I went to look at the sheep,
But I only had a little peep.
I went to see the goats,
But they were stranded in a moat.
I went to see the goose,
But it had broken loose.
I went to see a horse,
But he was running a racing course
And last of all I saw the farmer's dog
And he was sleeping right by a log.
It was the best day I've ever had.

Chloe Stiles (10)
Deddington CE Primary School

EGYPT

I can feel the really hot sand
I can taste nice fresh dates
I hear the vulture
Screaming for its prey
I smell the clear air
I take a step into the tomb
I see the hieroglyphs
As they come alive.

Barney Chadwick (8)
Deddington CE Primary School

HOLIDAYS

You fly, sail or travel in the car, it seems so far!
France, Spain, USA,
Wherever you are you can have a nice stay.
You can go to the seaside which is very sunny,
Covering people in sand, that's funny!
The smells are sweet and the water's cold,
I saw a man who was completely bald.
Playing bat and ball in the scorching sun,
Eating lunch, look I've got sand in my bun!
Oh no, it's nearly time to go,
It was hot at the seashore,
I want to go there more.
I'm going to miss the sea,
It's been an excellent time for me!

Nick Worrell (8)
Deddington CE Primary School

KEEP AWAY FROM SMILEY DON

Wimble, womble, pin, pick, pon
Keep away from smiley Don
His teeth are sharp, his scales are green,
He is hardly ever seen,
Until you stray too near,
He'll eat you up
With a laugh and a sneer.
So . . .
Wimble, womble, pin, pick, pon
Keep away from smiley Don.

Jonah Wimbush (10)
Deddington CE Primary School

CARS

Fast cars, slow cars, cool cars,
I like them all, convertibles, hatchbacks, saloons,
You name it, I've got it.
I like cars with elegance,
I like bangers, I like any cars that you can get,
Ford, Ferrari, Mercedes-Benz, I like them all.
Fast cars, slow cars, cool cars,
I love them all, you name them, I love them!

Joshua Allison (9)
Deddington CE Primary School

THE MUSEUM

I can see statues standing like soldiers
They are standing very straight
I can hear people running really fast
It sounds like rushing
I can touch hard walls
It feels like tile walls
I can smell rotten bread
It smells horrible.

Holly Boulter (8)
Deddington CE Primary School

IN THE TOMB

I see the glint of gold treasures.
I hear a creaking of a coffin opening.
I feel the walls as I go along.
I smell the dust tickling my nose.
I taste the cobwebs flying into my mouth.

Chelsea Tyler (7)
Deddington CE Primary School

THE TOMB

I can see the glint of a tomb,
It is light, like the sun shining.
I can hear the faint of noise of a tomb opening.
It sounds like a mummy walking.
I can feel the bumpy bandages of a mummy.
I feel the hard, cold statue,
It smells like a mouldy mummy.
I can taste the dusty air of a tomb.

Amber Broadwood (7)
Deddington CE Primary School

MY CAT

My cat is a lazy cat
All he does is sleep
He sits on the sofa and tries to bite your feet
My cat is a lazy cat
All he does is sleep
He goes around looking for lovely, juicy meat.

Nicola Isted (10)
Deddington CE Primary School

CATS

I crawl around all day
Creeping, searching for my prey
Then I leap into the air
I've got my dinner, a delicious hare.

Molly Davies (8)
Deddington CE Primary School

SWAN, DON'T GO AWAY

Swan, don't go away
Swan, swan, don't fly away
We want you to stay
Along the river you go
So steady and slow
Feathers like snow
Remember not to go

Swan, swan, don't go away
We'd love you to stay
Please don't go
Oh no
Now you've gone
I'll listen to the sparrow's song.

Siobhan Humphries (8)
Deddington CE Primary School

EXPLORING THE TOMB

I smell a mummy,
I smell old, dusty bones.
I feel the grit tumbling to the ground.
I touch the rough walls,
Working my way round the tomb.
I feel cold pottery, maybe a dish.
I light my torch,
I see golden chairs
And then a 3000-year-old mummy
Looking at me.

Thomas Salt (8)
Deddington CE Primary School

I'M LYING IN MY BED

I'm lying in my bed
There's a pain in my tummy -
A thought in my head

I'm lying in my bed
Shall I get up -
Or lie here instead?

I'm lying in my bed
It seems very dark -
I'll hold onto Ted!

I'm lying in my bed
Oh no -
A puddle the size of the Med!

Rachael Winter (8)
Deddington CE Primary School

THE EGYPTIAN LIFE

I can see a pyramid
It is huge and pointy
I can hear the wind
It is extremely sandy
I feel the pyramid
It is smooth and old
I smell the dead sand
It smells old and musty
I taste the bread
It is gritty and horrible.

Edward Preece (7)
Deddington CE Primary School

HEAR THIS!

Hear the croaking of the frogs,
Hear the barking of the dogs.
Hear the donkeys stamp and bray,
Hear the mice in the hay.
Hear the snapping of the twigs,
Hear the grunting of the pigs.
Hear the splashing in the lake,
Hear the quacking of the drake.

Elenya McGovern (8)
Deddington CE Primary School

THE TOMB

I can taste the gritty bread
It is hard in my mouth
I can feel the dusty cobwebs
It is sticking to my hands
I can hear the mummies talking
In their heads
I can smell the torch burning
I can see the tomb
All hard.

Siân Murphy (8)
Deddington CE Primary School

ON MY TRIP TO THE ZOO

Elephants, camels, hippos too
And pandas as well, eating bamboo.
Peacocks, geese and an owl,
Then I saw a dog being dried with a towel
On my trip to the zoo.

There was a rhino
And I saw a lizard you know.
There were mice and rats
And cats wearing hats
On my trip to the zoo.

Jennie Hovard (10)
Deddington CE Primary School

THE TOMB

Dusty cobwebs brush, brush, brushing against my face,
The dirty sand blow, blow, blowing towards me.
The bright, blinding gold shines, shines, shining.
The rot, rot, rotting of a mummy.
The walls crumb, crumb, crumbling.
The mummy talk, talk, talking,
I don't know if it's real . . .

Effie Alton (8)
Deddington CE Primary School

THE TOMB

I can see the mummy,
It is creepy, horrible and still.
I can hear an archaeologist,
He is talking, still and quiet.
I can feel the wall,
It is bumpy, crumply and hard.
I can smell gold,
It is salty and stinky.
I can taste the cobwebs,
They are yucky and rotten.

Jordan Brady (7)
Deddington CE Primary School

IN A TOMB

I can see nothing because it's dark,
I need a torch to see.

I can feel a large, smooth box,
It has patterns and pictures of people all over.

I can smell a burning torch and dust,
I can taste the dust in my mouth.

Thomas Rollason (8)
Deddington CE Primary School

THE TOMB

I enter the tomb
And feel the pressure
Of ancient air
I can smell the rotten death of mummies
It smells dusty and of slate
I can taste the gritty sand
Like flaky gravel
I feel goosebumps on my skin
I hear my heart drum.

Josh Rackley (8)
Deddington CE Primary School

TOMBS

I can see the mummies
Still as a rock
I hear the walls
Crumbling onto the floor
I can feel the stone

Of the coffins
I smell the rotting walls
Of the tombs
I taste the gritty sand
In my mouth.

Adam Taylor (7)
Deddington CE Primary School

MUSEUM

I see the 3000-year-old bread
It is black with lots of stones, sand and dirt in it
I hear the cabinet crashing in the dark, gloomy night
It sounds like footsteps moving
I feel the cabinet rocking
While I'm walking through the museum
It feels like the roof falling
I smell dirty things
It smells like dirty floors.

Ross Gardner (8)
Deddington CE Primary School

MY POEM

I've got to write a poem
But I don't know what to write
Jimmy's done his dog
Maddie's done my hair
Everyone thinks I'll do just great
But if I do, I won't be proud of it
I'd think that it's been a mistake
Hey, wait a minute
This would be just great.

Evelyn Cook (9)
Deddington CE Primary School

SNOW DAY

S   now day is here again, what shall I do?
N   ow I'll build snowmen, lots of them, hooray.
O   w, I got hit by a snowball, I'm having so much fun.
W   ell I'll be a snow-queen, so beautiful and fair,
     I'll have a castle so tall, nobody will climb it, nobody at all.

D   ay coming to an end, still 5 hours, that's OK
A   nd the day has been so much fun, I hope it'll never end.
Y   our turn to have a snow day and my turn for bed.

Danielle Fairns (10)
Deddington CE Primary School

SCHOOL AND MUD DON'T MIX

'Not again Ben, you have mud everywhere.'
'I know, Mum, it was done by a bear.'
'No, don't lie, I can see right through.'
'OK, I fell in a puddle by the zoo.'
'But . . .' said Lucy.
'Don't,' said Ben.
'Have you been playing in the mud again?'
'OK, I have.'
Now I'm in a fix,
School and mud just don't mix.

Charlotte Hawkins (10)
Deddington CE Primary School

MY GARDEN

In my garden the roses grow high,
With massive thorns and resting butterflies.
The grass, juicy green, blowing in the breeze,
The leaves on the oak tree, happy and free.
I like my garden
Because the roses grow high,
With my special butterflies.
My garden has that happy look,
That breezy air and I like it
Because it is mine!

George Richards (9)
Deddington CE Primary School

FORMULA ONE

My favourite is Arrows,
Well some like Benetton,
Some like Ferrari,
Some like BAR,
Some like McLaren,
Some like Prost,
People like Jordan,
Some like Williams,
But, well to be honest,
I love all of them!

Lewis Taylor (9)
Deddington CE Primary School

OPENING A TOMB

I can see the faint glint of a gold mummy
It is a light like the sun
I can hear my footsteps in the grit
It is creepy, I think the spirit has come alive
I can feel the crumbly walls beneath my hands
It is vanishing
I can smell the sandy air
It is in my eyes
I can taste the ceiling sprinkling on my face
It tickles me.

Stephanie Bolduc (8)
Deddington CE Primary School

MY DAY

Horses stand strong
And they pong.
I sing them a sweet song,
Which is very, very long.
The horses fight,
With all their might.
When they charge, I run,
Which is a lot of fun.
When it's home time,
I eat a lovely bun in the sun.
Then my mum says, 'Go to bed,'
Having a full tum.

Flo Davenport (10)
Deddington CE Primary School

My Chaotic Journey Home

'In you get then, into the car.'
'How long will it take? Is it far?'
'Are you asleep Finn or are you awake?'
'OK, you lot, do you want crisps or cake?'
'How long have I been asleep, two hours or four?'
At the services now, can't open the door!
Time for an ice cream, hey only one lick!
To the toilet quick for I'm feeling sick!
'Stop hitting me Ceara, stop pulling my hair!'
'He had four sweets, that's not fair!'
On the ceiling, making dents in the foam,
Yes, we've made it, at last we're home!

Briony Martin (10)
Finstock CE Primary School

One Foggy Night

On a dark and foggy night,
The bathroom light was dim,
I heard a crash
And then a splash,
Good god!
She's fallen in!

Craig Wood (11)
Finstock CE Primary School

THE JOURNEY TO MARS . . .

The journey to Mars . . .
Grandma's.
The long journey
Makes the picture of her
Loaded with lipstick
And ready to kiss even worse.
Now I'm feeling sick,
Partly because I hate lipstick
And partly because the journey is one
Big roller coaster.
At least it gives me an excuse to dash off
When we get there.
Oh no,
We're there.
I'm going in,
'One small step for man,
One terrible nightmare for a ten-year-old boy.'

Adam Sambrook (11)
Finstock CE Primary School

THE VOLCANO

Rumbling and shaking ground,
Lava falls running down, down, down,
Rushing down to the ground,
Hot rains of ash,
Fiery magma, dangerous and powerful,
Burying everything in its path,
Magma sleeps and the volcano rests.

Lauren Janson (8)
Glory Farm CP School

THE JUMPING RABBIT

R unning free all around, jumping and dancing
A ll different kinds of rabbits or hares
B ig and small, short and tall
B right colours and dull
I t is strange why they run away
T hey have tall ears and short
S ome are babies as well

R umbling through the soil to find a home
A bout ten in a family
B attered and bruised they can e
B ad and good they might be
I t is fun to have them as pets
T hey can run very fast
S ome are babies as well

That's rabbits!

Katie Lodge (8)
Glory Farm CP School

WINTER

Pale moon in the skylight
Glittering with all its might
Snowflakes prancing in the air
Round the trees that are bare

Warm and cosy in the house
Not a sound, not even a mouse
It's Christmas Eve, we're so excited
In the morning we'll be delighted.

Daniel Sutton (9)
Glory Farm CP School

ALL FOUR SEASONS

Winter's here, it's cold and bleak,
The wind blows hard against my cheek,
There's a candle in the window,
It flickers in the dark,
The trees are bare, they've lost their leaves,
All that's left is bark.

Buds are beginning to sprout,
Soon flowers will start to pop out,
Baby animals are being born,
If we're lucky, we may see a fawn.

Summer is hot, warm and sunny,
It makes my ice cream all gooey and runny,
I play games on the beach and bury Dad in the sand,
Holidays are great, in fact they're just grand.

Autumn time has come,
You don't see much now of the sun,
Leaves are changing colours, from green to gold,
Winter's on its way, *brrr* it's getting cold!

Hannah Greenhalgh (9)
Glory Farm CP School

UNTITLED

The mountain stands there really high,
At the top it touches the sky,
Some have snow and ice,
People climb right up,
Lots of crumply rocks are on the top,
Very pointy and very cold.

Yasmeen Ward (8)
Glory Farm CP School

SEASONS

Spring is when the animals and baby birds are born,
When farmers start to grow their corn,
As snowdrops and daffodils fade away,
Spring starts to end its day.

Summer is time to run and play,
Horses start to stamp and neigh,
You don't need much shade,
As summer begins to fade.

Autumn is when the leaves turn gold,
Yellow, brown, orange and red,
Autumn starts to grab its hold,
As winter wants to go ahead.

Winter is the coldest part of the year,
With snowmen and Christmas,
Winter is over but . . .
A new year has begun!

Eleanor Deeley (9)
Glory Farm CP School

DROUGHT

The sun's been shining
For days and days,
Making everything hot,
With its golden rays.

The river got so hot,
The water went away,
Now Pooh and Piglet
Can't go fishing today.

Jake Holden (8)
Glory Farm CP School

UNTITLED

Boom!
Boiling lava rushing down,
Crushing buildings like it doesn't care,
Burning the houses in the town,
Melting the fun, noisy fairs,
Black sky from the ash,
Rock breaking off and making a crash.

Tom Heasley (8)
Glory Farm CP School

BOOM!

Boiling lava racing down
The volcano to the bare ground
Destroying anything in its way
Explosions happening all around
And all the ash is grey
There is a very horrible sound.

David Aslett (9)
Glory Farm CP School

VOLCANO

Crash!
Lava flowing down and down,
Lava flowing towards a town,
People evacuated from their homes,
When people go, all they do is moan.

Liam Bowdidge (9)
Glory Farm CP School

THE BEACH

The lapping waves washing me away,
The blowing sand glittering so bright,
The beautiful trees growing so wide,
The loud people happily playing,
Shining rocks glittering with joy,
The burning sun shining bright-yellow.

Abby Seger (7)
Glory Farm CP School

THE DESERT

In the desert it is boiling hot,
The sand is yellow,
Beautiful deserts,
Deserts have deep, dark skies,
Colours spread across the sky,
Orange, red, yellow, pink and blue.

Harriet Wall (7)
Glory Farm CP School

LANDSCAPE POEM

The stones as grey as a path
The river as cold as ice
The grass as green as leaves
The wood as brown as a dog
What is it?
Landscape.

Arlo Union (7)
Glory Farm CP School

THE KARATE COW

There once was a very peculiar cow
Who lived in a shed and his name was Pow
The reason why it had a weird name
Was because it was really insane
And it did karate moves
Plus dancing grooves

One day it entered a wrestling ring
To take on an elephant called Sting
The elephant thought to make a bet
That he would get the strange cow's pet
So the cow used its karate moves
And the elephant used its ninja grooves

The elephant smacked it with its leg
And the cow was just about to beg
But the cow used a karate chop
Putting the elephant to a stop.

Dominic Blossom (9)
Glory Farm CP School

TOYS

Toys, toys, toys, nothing but toys,
Nothing in here for boys,
I've got to get rid of these toys,
There are too many in my room.
I'll sweep them with a broom,
I just can't stand these toys,
Take them out boys,
That's got rid of those toys.

Sophie Bushnell (8)
Glory Farm CP School

OUR SCHOOL

This is a poem about our school,
It's got great teachers and it's really cool.

Our head teacher is called Mr Waine,
But he's very friendly and doesn't complain.

Our teacher, Mrs Chodyniecki has a dog called Molly,
Her nickname is Mad Mol which is really funny.

Sometimes we are allowed to bring in toys,
Which means there's going to be a lot of noise.

We mess about in the classroom all day,
Until we are let out to play.

At break time we shout and play,
It's really tiring at the end of the day.

That was a poem about our school,
It's got great teachers and it's really cool.

Laura Gladdy (9)
Glory Farm CP School

WATERFALL

Waterfall, waterfall,
Bubbling to the river,
Sparkling in the light,
Jumping over rocks,
With a dither,
With the sun shining bright,
Peacefully people watch.

Sophie Jones (9)
Glory Farm CP School

THE BEACH

The sparkly waves lapping and hitting the shore
Like a giant hand,
Glittering sand twinkling in the night,
The beautiful sunset blazing down at me,
Noisy people having fun and playing happily,
Some licking ice cream to cool them down,
Feel the breeze touch your skin
As you run and play about,
Smell the coconut in the air
And the salty sea,
Hundreds of creatures,
Different sizes like glittery starfish.

Daphne Peart (8)
Glory Farm CP School

LANDSCAPE POEM

Lily pad floating on a stream,
Frog jumping one, two, three,
Eating bugs for their tea.

Ducks quacking, a noisy sound,
Ducking their heads up and down,
Eating bread that's left around.

Fish are swimming in and out
The reeds and plants that move,
Looking for some tasty food.

Hayley Anderson (9)
Glory Farm CP School

DOLPHINS

Dolphins are cute and really sweet,
They are definitely a creature you would like to meet,
They like to swim in the deep blue pool,
They are totally wicked and really cool.

Dolphins are loving and very caring,
They like swimming and sharing,
Dolphins are very graceful,
They like to play and they're wonderful.

Dolphins are colourful,
They are also delightful,
Dolphins like to have fun
And they like getting things done.

Rebecca North (9)
Glory Farm CP School

THE WEATHER

W ind is a really strong breeze
E   ven enough to start to freeze
A   t the winter months and time
T   he trees are all covered with slime
H   ot it is in the sun
E   at a pink iced bun
R   ain is a wet thing

T   hat's the time to go in
I   t is great in the sun
M e and you have some fun
E   ager to see the weather.

Jamie Swanson (8)
Glory Farm CP School

SADIE THE DOG OF WONDERS

S he is black and white
A s dark as the night on a full moon
D ownstairs she will roam
I f she hears a noise she will bark and bark
E ven if there's nobody there

T welve past one, she'll go to sleep
H esitating at every second
E veryone knows they're safe

D rowning in a deep, deep sleep
O f horrors around her
G rowling at nothing, just her nightmare

O ccasionally she'll come upstairs
F ighting to tackle the cracks in the floorboards

W hining to everyone to get a space on the bed
O ut of the room Sadie will go
N ibbling her bottom lip
D own back to her chair
E arly in the morning she'll wake up
R unning into the kitchen for food
S cratching all the cupboards.

Sarah Humphries (8)
Glory Farm CP School

JEALOUSY

Jealousy is a dark corner,
Sitting in a dark shadow,
Dreaming in a dark world,
Where nobody can find you.

Then you see a patch of light,
Leading you up and onwards,
To lead you out of jealousy
And bring you back to life.

Bethan Jeacock (9)
Glory Farm CP School

THE MONKEY

Passing trees,
With bumblebees,
Climbing high,
Swinging high.

Colour brown,
Like a funny clown,
Climbing high,
Swinging high.

Running around,
With an ooo-eee sound,
Climbing high,
Swinging high.

Light brown eyes,
With red-hot skies,
Climbing high,
Swinging high.

Looks for food,
With a good mood,
Climbing high,
Swinging high.

Liam Phipps (8)
Glory Farm CP School

THE DRAGON

Inside a dark cave full of spiderwebs like glittering light strings
Lives a creature giant, winged, fire-breathing lizard.
A giant, deadly lizard known as a dragon.
It breathes red-hot flames like glittery red paper flapped by the wind.
Scales bright like a polished marble floor.
Claws like knives.
Feasts on people.
The dragon exterminates anything in its path.
It breathes fire, destroying the towns it lives near.
Although not real, still scares people.
If true, knights fighting,
But no, only in our imagination this creature lives,
But who knows, it may live!

Jack Little (8)
Glory Farm CP School

THE WATERFALL

Hitting the rocks as it hurries down
If you feel in the bottom, you're likely to drown
The rocks are all green, all covered in moss
The rocks are all slippery if you try to cross
Hitting the bottom as it sprays all round
Making me wet and soaking the ground
Rainbow clouds appear in the sky
As ducks and geese go flying by
Night comes back in the starry sky
And the end of the waterfall starts to cry.

Daniel Wilson (9)
Glory Farm CP School

RABBIT

R   ushing round the garden, up and down on their feet
A   dvances through the prickly bushes
B   obbling fluffy tails as soft and cute as could be
B   itsy-witsy face all so cuddly and tincy
I   tsy-bitsy ears so soft as a tissue and baggy as can be
T   witching furry toes like a cotton ball.

Sophie Trinder (8)
Glory Farm CP School

GO AND OPEN THE WINDOW

Go and open the window
Maybe there's a frog dawdling
A dog rummaging
Or a monkey dangling

Go and open the window
Maybe there's a tulip singing,
A daisy dancing
Or a daffodil swimming

Go and open the window
Maybe there's an appetising smell
Of wonderful food
Or the bake of a cake

Go and open the window
If there's a storm
It will pass.

Amy Santos (9)
Glory Farm CP School

MY DOG

B   arney is very furry
A   nd really kind
R   ound the corner he chases cats
N   evertheless he jumps with fright
E   njoys delicious food
Y   ou can't get away from his din

T   ears come down when he cries
H   e likes to run
E   verybody likes him

D   oes not bite anyone
O   ver he jumps if you've
G   ot some dogs, he will get them.

Kyle Price (8)
Glory Farm CP School

PEPSI

P   layful
E   yes like diamonds
P   aws that are soft
S   mooth fur
I   love them when they bark

T   ail wagging madly
H   elp, she's chasing me
E   ars flop up and down

D   igging in the garden
O   ver the hedge
G   rinning when naughty.

Sophie Beard (8)
Glory Farm CP School

SHETLAND PONIES

Shetland ponies are quiet and strong
And never, never do anything wrong
They're cute and soft and cuddly too
And I just wish they could come home with me and you

Their sparkling eyes gleam with power
And after rolling in the mud they have a shower
I like white Shetland ponies best
But I also like all the rest

They have lots of friends, that's good
And eat all their food and drink like they should
They're graceful and dainty all day
And all I want to do is play, play, play.

Rebecca Landy (9)
Glory Farm CP School

THE BEACH

A beach is sandy and rocky
A beach is dry
The sea is calm and blue
The hot sunshine shining on people
The calm sea moving from side to side
The loud people happily playing on the beach
People sunbathing under the sparkly sun
As the sparkly sun was about to set
The deep blue sky transformed into bright purple
The wind started to change the calm sea
Into bright patterns
The sea, miles away from the beach.

Emma Strong (7)
Glory Farm CP School

FLOWERS

There are some lovely flowers
Which are so pretty
Here are some roses and posies which are everywhere
You can see all the flowers which are pretty colours from far, faraway
You could want all of them

On top of the hill where they all are
There are different flowers on the hill
Different flowers, different colours all around you.

Alice King (8)
Glory Farm CP School

THE VOLCANO

As the vicious volcano's starting to burn,
Burning, bustling volcano
Sizzling volcano like the deep blue ocean
Volcanoes are dangerous
Like a glowing ball of fire.

Joshua Gibbs (8)
Glory Farm CP School

DAISY

My cat's called Daisy
She is always laying in daisies
Daisy is like Hazy
They are both so lazy
And Daisy is my cat.

Rebecca Moore (9)
Glory Farm CP School

FLUFFY SNOW-CAPPED MOUNTAIN

Fluffy snow-capped mountain
Soft, cold snow like a freezer
A mountain of ice
Like ice cream
White, blue, creamy and fluffy,
Bumpy, rough surfaces all over the place.

Carl Marchant (7)
Glory Farm CP School

CATS

My cat's name is called Maze
She likes to play with a paper chain
My cat, Maze she loves to roll
In lots of daises
She likes to play with other cats
And she sleeps on our mats
My cat, Maze is mine!

Emma Teall (8)
Glory Farm CP School

VOLCANO

V   olcanoes are boiling hot
O   pen up like a rocket
L   ava pours out
C   ountryside is scared to death
A   ll of the houses have gone
N   ow it has stopped
O   ther things have gone.

Joseph Dixey (8)
Glory Farm CP School

THE QUEEN

The Queen has been on her throne for 50 years,
Sometimes with happiness,
Sometimes with tears.
All around the world she goes,
I feel sorry for the servants, they have to carry loads.
As she stepped into the carriage, her jewels gleamed,
Her crown was on her head, she looked like a dream.
She has two Corgis which she walks on a lead,
When she was young, she rode a valiant steed.

J'nae Saunders (8)
Glory Farm CP School

CLOUDY BEACH

Look, look at the hills under a chalky mist
Near crashing waves;
Near frothy, crashing waves
And dark, dark clouds,
Look, look at the farmers feeding the lambs,
Staring across the dark, dark land,
Look, look at the seagulls
Swooping across the dark, dark sky
Look, just look, shh!

Kerrie-Anne Price (7)
Glory Farm CP School

FRIENDS

Friends are always there for you,
They never let you down,
If you're hurt, they will help you,
If you are sad they will make you happy,
They might be your friend forever.

Friends are so kind to you,
You will want to be their friend
And never hate them and never lie,
Your friendship might not last forever,
In your life.

Robert Atkins (9)
Glory Farm CP School

THE KING

He's the beast, looking sly as he pounces on his prey,
Slowly walks nearer and nearer,
Waiting, being terrified as hunters try to track him down.

As he creeps around his prey,
The birds are dying every second,
He's got him, flesh and blood everywhere.

His paws are like knives,
His royal crown, his royal fur,
He's full,
Left there, the animal lays.

Hannah Titchener (9)
Glory Farm CP School

THE BEACH

A sandy beach that people play on
Some hard rocks that people sit on
A lovely sound from people
Lapping waves coming over me
The beautiful trees shining out at me
Loud people calling at me.

Demi Coleman (8)
Glory Farm CP School

THE LION

He is prowling through the long grass
Looking for his prey
There are trees and lovely golden grass around him
In the distance he sees his prey
A nice, juicy buffalo drinking from the watering hole
He is running towards the prey
It spots him and runs so fast that a human couldn't catch it
Finally the buffalo is caught and the lion digs in.

Jessica Kempster (8)
Glory Farm CP School

THE LION

Stalking in the wild trees,
Waiting for his prey,
Here comes the king of the jungle,
Marching throughout the day,
Holding up his royal mane,
Showing the animals proudly,
Here comes his prey, the deer,
Run, pounce and eat.

Daniel Howlett (9)
Glory Farm CP School

THE DESERT

A desert is rocky and hot,
The dry ground is glittering,
The sun is setting,
The sand is changing patterns.

Christopher Troth (7)
Glory Farm CP School

A VOLCANO

The hot lava sizzling and shooting out of the top,
The dangerous lava flooding towns,
It is like a dinosaur biting through villages and towns,
Lava is bubbling a dark brown, nasty red,
Yellow and orange are the main colours of lava,
It is like a big high mountain painted with a light brown,
The vicious mountain will be shooting out lava any moment.

Emily Baker (8)
Glory Farm CP School

LANDSCAPE POEM

The burning sun making you sizzle
Like a sausage
The sand blowing in the wind
With the relaxing whistling wind
Releasing patterns across the desert
Then freshly cooked sand burns you.

Steven Davidson (7)
Glory Farm CP School

THE HILLS

When the bright sun goes to sleep,
The field fills with purple light,
All the sheep go to sleep
And red poppies bloom all around,
The wind blows freshly cut grass
And the farmer settles down to sleep.

Nicholle Hornsby (8)
Glory Farm CP School

THE LION

His powerful paws
Tear through the long, stringy grass
Stalking his prey
In his dry, sandy shrub lands
Surrounded by huge rocks and long grass
Far in the distance he hears a noise
And as fast as a lightning bolt
He tears to a heard of giant water buffalo
Near his watering hole.

James Gwyn (8)
Glory Farm CP School

THE DRAGON

He, the dragon, strong, fierce, ready to fight,
He breathes fire like the burning sun,
He flies like a mad eagle.

Houses surrounding him all around,
He looks like an ugly bug,
He doesn't give up.

Wade Tallis (8)
Glory Farm CP School

THE VOLCANO

Thick lava running through the town,
All is covered in lava, brown,
Dark red and dark orange burst from the volcano,
Its colours spreading across the land.

Robert McGregor (7)
Glory Farm CP School

THE FALCON

He looks round with a small black eye,
Then he spots a rat in the distance,
Like a caught mouse he shrieks.

He drops like a lightning bolt
And kills the rat in an instant,
He is now eating his prey.

Matthew Sherwood (9)
Glory Farm CP School

MY RABBIT

My rabbit is called Dapple
She had an apple
An apple she had today
She's had a rest
She looks her best
And now she's ready to play.

Jasmin Whiteford (8)
Glory Farm CP School

VOLCANOES

Thick, oozy lava
Red, orange, yellow
Boiling hot magma
Flowing down the mountain
To destroy the village
Throwing out lava
Destroying the land.

Joshua Keith (8)
Glory Farm CP School

THE LION

Waiting for his prey to arrive
He creeps in the field
Then suddenly he hears a rustling
Sound in the distance
He goes to see what it is
It's what he's been waiting for
Then suddenly he pounces
And runs as fast as he possibly can
He runs like a lightning bolt.

Bethany Hewitt (8)
Glory Farm CP School

THE POND SKIER

Down by the pond,
Skiing high, skiing low.

A pond insect returns,
Skiing high, skiing low.

Everybody watches him,
Skiing high, skiing low.

Toddlers come up and say hello,
Skiing high, skiing low.

Lauren Stanford (8)
Glory Farm CP School

DON'T DO DRUGS AND ALCOHOL

D on't do drugs and alcohol they will give you grief all your life long
O h no, someone's dead from doing drugs and alcohol
N ow it's time to put a stop to all those drugs and most of the alcohol
T each all those who do them not to take them anymore and help them to live

D rugs are in alcohol, put them together and you will be dead
O n the scale teenagers are the worst at doing them

D itch the drugs and alcohol, put a ban to it all
R andom drugs can be found all over the world
U nder drugs you will die from taking them
G ood not to take them if you want to live
S un makes you dehydrate when you drink alcohol

A nymore taking them and the whole world will die
N ow it's time to give them up
D rugs are dangerous things to take

A lcohol is bad for you
L ike it you should not
C ome out of doing drugs and alcohol
O h so bad for you to take
H ome you go, Mum knows you've been on the booze, your mum shuts you out
O n the block your mum puts you for doing the booze
L ink the alcohol and drugs together, you will be dead in a minute or two.

Jessica Tuffrey (9)
Glory Farm CP School

THE LIONS

Lions are strong and powerful
They roar as loud as an earthquake
They are very determined
Waiting for their prey

They're watching their prey
And then it runs away
And the lion dashes after it.

Michael (8)
Glory Farm CP School

TV

My TV likes fantastic action films
Not boring news
My TV likes dramatic drama
Not soppy sad films
My TV likes comic comedy shows

My TV works hard with the aerial
To find what we want
And it doesn't always like what he finds
So at night, he turns himself on
And watches what he wants to watch

He has the time of his life
Playing videos and eating electrical wires
He puts on his favourite films
The funniest shows and then . . .
We unplug him!

Matthew Crook (10)
Kings Meadow Primary School

SCHOOL

Children hate their days at school,
Most of them that is,
Some of them are shy and quiet,
Others a science whizz.
Teachers are both strict and nice,
They like to play about,
On the playground they have rules,
Kids love to scream and shout.
English, maths and science,
The main subjects of the day,
Teachers tell them what to do,
But kids like to have their own way!

Sophie Yazdi (10)
Kings Meadow Primary School

TIGER KENNING

Prey catcher
Angry snatcher
Grass cruncher
Midnight scruncher
Loud snarler
Petrifying gnarler
Silent creeper
Long sleeper
Blood lover
Stripy cover
Good hider
No guider
Super glider.

Zoe Gordon (10)
Kings Meadow Primary School

WIND

I am wind,
I knock clouds together
And summon lightning.
I pull heads off flowers,
Tear branches off trees.
I terrorise leaves,
Shaking them to death.
I spin smoke from chimneys,
I beat rain
Against windowpanes,
Making them rattle and groan.
I make the sea churn
And smash against rocks,
Spraying the seagulls with foam.
I swirl dust and rubbish
Into corners,
I scrunch faces up
And throw hats into the sky.
Once I have caused chaos,
I feel out of breath.
With the strength I have left,
I swiftly glide back
To my draughty cave
And wait for my strength to return.

Heather Luckhurst (10)
Kings Meadow Primary School

GOD

He clashes cymbals,
Moves furniture,
Spills bottles of water,
Sprinkles snowflakes across the land,
Throws a ball of fire in the air.

At night he throws silver glitter in the air
And a shining silver ball with them,
Picking up houses, chucking them across the land,
Dropping baseballs,
Making us sweat like mad.

Aaron Jell (8)
Kings Meadow Primary School

WIND

I am the wind
I throw leaves about
And make them shake and shiver
I blow rubbish into corners
I call for my brothers, thunder, lightning and hurricane
To do some more damage

I still thrash and batter things
I start whipping up chilly winds in people's faces
Children start to whine and cry
I whistle through windows
I blow people's hair and make it a mess
I send sand into people's eyes

I send masses of wind to the Earth
I wrestle against the dark clouds
I cause the blizzards and the sandstorms
I hear chaos below me

Then suddenly I loose all my energy
There is silence again
I regain my energy and snap thin trees
And collapse, though I can't go any longer
And disappear.

Dipesh Mistry (10)
Kings Meadow Primary School

FOG

I blanket the Earth,
I smother sight and muffle voices.
Everything smells musky in my breath,
Every time I breathe, I become thicker,
My mother is Faint Mist,
I come from her.
To Earth I am cold and a chaos-causer,
I crash cars and collide lorries,
I despise Sun,
I fight and battle her.
She drains my power,
We are mortal enemies.
I fade as Sun warms up the Earth,
She shreds me until there is nothing left,
But faint wisps of grey,
But I will rise again,
With the next full moon.

Danielle Howard (11)
Kings Meadow Primary School

MY DOG, JASPER

Jasper, Jasper, he's so cute
Always playing round people's feet
Chews all my socks and my boots
Whatever next shall he do?
He can be good some of the time
When he's playing round his friends and mine.

Chloe Anne Straiton (8)
Kings Meadow Primary School

WHAT A DAY ON THE BEACH

We were on the beach,
We three, Dad, Mum and me.
I was bored,
My dad said, 'Do you want to come on a walk with me?'
I said, 'No thanks.'
He had taken about three steps,
When he said, 'Can you pass me some paper and a pen.'
So I did. He took it and carried on his walk,
When he got back he gave me the paper and pen.
Dad said, 'It's a treasure map,
It doesn't take you long,' Dad said.
I started to follow the map to the end.
Before I got there, I stood on some rocks
And screamed, 'There's a crab under my foot.'
I looked down and saw rocks,
I went red in the face when everyone looked at me.
When I got there, it was a boat,
I looked inside the boat, it had silver and gold rubbish in.
I got back to Mum and Dad
And I told them that the treasure was wonderful.

Katie Brown (9)
Kings Meadow Primary School

MY DOG, BARNEY

Barney
Sweet, shy
My dog, Barney
Big, strong and handsome
Alert, also cute and cuddly
Mischievous, funny, playful, intelligent and smart
Barney!

Rebecca Train (8)
Kings Meadow Primary School

I SEE A CUNNING PIGEON

I see a cunning pigeon,
Gliding from side to side,
Watching carefully,
Aiming at a target,
Skilfully landing,
Secretly hiding,
Stealthily creeping,
Slowly coming,
Slyly moving in.

I see a cunning pigeon,
Swooping down for prey,
Beautifully swaying,
Pale grey,
Body wide and stretched,
Skin as smooth as a baby,
Silently concentrating,
Waits until his prey is still,
Quietly but quickly - pecks!

Daniel Crook (8)
Kings Meadow Primary School

HORSE

I see a small, quiet horse,
Eating fresh, green grass.
It is moving very slowly
Through the field,
She is a white colour,
The shape of its body is oval,
The fur is silky,
It is drinking and playing cheerfully.

Gemma Sweetman (8)
Kings Meadow Primary School

KETCHUP ON CORNFLAKES

Do you like ketchup on cornflakes?
Would you like a brown mud tea?
Would you like a ham, mounted with jam,
With seaweed from under the sea?

Do you like ketchup on cornflakes,
With a squirt from the mustard pot?
Would you like some bread with some slimy, green spread,
On some cheese that had started to rot?

Do you like ketchup on cornflakes
Or do you really think it's quite grim?
Slugs on toast or do you prefer roast?
Has you stomach begun to kick in?

Connie Hollyer (10)
Kings Meadow Primary School

PRESENTS

Presents are square,
Presents are round,
Presents to share,
Some never found.
Everyone loves them,
Paper to rip,
Like a sparkling gem,
Some have a zip.
Some under the tree,
A couple for me,
Some for a birthday,
Hip hip hooray!

Jessica Scott (9)
Kings Meadow Primary School

MY FURRY FRIEND

In two years
We're all in tears
These are the thing he likes to do best
As he stays away from being depressed
Because he's a
Ball roller
A day stroller
Oh! He's a
House raider
And a night cascader
He's a
Party pooper
Cheek drooper
A
Treat nibbler
Water dribbler
Lazy creature
An amazing feature
With teeth that are yellow, he's a real cute fellow
His name's taken after a double whammy
For he's my pet, my hamster called Hammy.

Thomas Smith (10)
Kings Meadow Primary School

THERE WAS AN OLD LADY FROM WALES

There was an old lady from Wales,
Who liked to go out in the gales,
She was walking round one day,
When the gales took her away,
That strange old lady from Wales.

Laura Burchell (10)
Kings Meadow Primary School

UNDERWATER CREATURES

Vicious sharks swim through the sea,
Rainbowfish come and follow me,
Some strange little catfish as they stare into space,
Small, little pupils look into a face,
A face with some warming, fiery eyes,
Next to a face full of hatred and lies.

A stingray swims across the land,
As crabs shuffle across the sand,
The rocks are heavy and stay underground,
At the bottom of the ocean where you won't hear a sound.
If you want to see some marvellous seals,
Then you better watch out for the electric eels.

Ellie Seddon (10)
Kings Meadow Primary School

MEAN OLD CATFISH

I see an old, slumped catfish
Minding his own business, swimming
Looking for his food
Moving as slow as a lazy snail
Crawling through ten-foot grass
As dark as a plimsoll in the moonlight
His body the shape of a tiny circle
With dangerous spikes
Making the sound of wind through rocks
Waiting for silent carp
So if you go in the sea - *look out!*

Lewis Gordon (9)
Kings Meadow Primary School

THERE WAS AN OLD MAN FROM BATH

There was an old man from Bath
Who came here and just wanted to laugh
He thought it was funny
That he had no money
That weird old man from Bath.

Melissa Hawkes-Blackburn (9)
Kings Meadow Primary School

FIRE

I am a house destroyer!
A mega house taker!
My friends are the wind and the sun.
I am hot,
I am bright,
I am furious,
I am a life taker!
I am fire!

Charlie Sutcliffe (7)
Kings Meadow Primary School

FRIENDS

We've broken up,
We've asked if we can make up.
We want to be friends
And friends we will be.
But if we're not,
Then that's the lot.
So let's be friends!

Maddison Butler (8)
Kings Meadow Primary School

I SEE A STRIPY DOG

I see a stripy dog,
Chasing a ginger cat,
Moving very quickly,
Black, grey, small and thin,
Fur soft,
Panting and barking,
Leaping in the air,
Racing round his garden delightedly.

Robyn Cook (8)
Kings Meadow Primary School

GALLOPING HORSEY

Horsey, horsey, don't you stop
Past Milly Maid and Curly Locks
You're going quite quickly
Gallopy, gallopy, go.

Sophie Bebb (6)
Kings Meadow Primary School

TIGER KENNING

Eye shiner
Fox catcher
Leg chopper
Meat eater
Mouse nicker
Bear chaser
Tail pincher
Prey snatcher
Lemming hunter.

Andrew Green (8)
Kings Meadow Primary School

MOBILE PHONE

Game player
Word sayer
Call maker
Easy breaker
No walker
Fast talker
Colour wearer
No tearer
Groovy keypad
No kneepad
Old new
Brown blue
People ringer
Smile bringer
No singer.

Chloe Davis (10)
Kings Meadow Primary School

MY DOG

I see a black dog
Growling and jumping up
Trying to get in
A dark-black Border collie
Black dog, thin, straight,
Skin smooth as baby's skin
Making a soft barking noise
Sleeping on the sofa.

Aimee Cross (9)
Kings Meadow Primary School

NIGHT

I am the night,
I arrive by sneaking, then I leap out,
Sending the day asleep!
After sunset I can control the whole world,
Anyone who comes in my path
Are cast into shadows,
I sit there holding and watching the stars,
Moon and planets,
My face lights up from the glowing moon,
My hair waves through the cold, windy air
And my eyes sparkle like stars,
I have owls flying and squealing
And I have hedgehogs silently creeping
Across every garden,
Night is the most powerful of them all,
But is defeated by a stroke of sunlight.

Robert Howkins (11)
Kings Meadow Primary School

A CHEEKY PARROT

I see a cheeky parrot
Cunningly copying what I say!
Silently, slowly moving away from me
Godly, orangey, yellow
Oval-shaped body
Cheeky, squeaking
Pecking your neck in annoyance
Whining pitifully when tired.

Rebecca Cross (9)
Kings Meadow Primary School

SNEEZES

I'd like to tell you a story
At least I think I do
It was when I had the flu
I was sitting with my mum
Not having much fun
When I sneezed, when I say I sneezed
I mean I sneezed
I could tell I was going to sneeze
My nose started running
My eyes were watering
And I could feel my eyes closing
I thought to myself
Oh! Here it comes
There it was, atchoo!
The biggest sneeze I'd ever done
Oh no! Here comes another
Atchoo!
And another
Atchoo!
And another
Atchoo!
Well, you could tell I had the flu.

Carianne Rudge (11)
Kings Meadow Primary School

SOMEONE

Someone scratched the leather sofa,
Someone scribbled on the wall,
Someone spilt cornflakes on the table,
Someone let a draught in through the door.

I have a feeling inside me,
That no one's going to like me,
When I tell them it was me all along.

Someone hugged me round the chest,
Someone kissed me on the cheek,
Someone said, 'I love you' when it was time for bed,
So I guess I was loved all along.

Rachel Cullup-Smith (10)
Kings Meadow Primary School

MY DAD (THE *BIG* KID)

My dad
Is extremely mad
You'll never guess what he did?

He climbed on the shed top,
With a big bunny-hop
And said, 'Aye, aye, look at me,
I can see right out to sea!'

Then with an elastic band,
Tied 5 twigs onto each hand,
'I'm an X-man,
Wolverine's the name,
Don't worry, I'll save you Jean Grey!'

Next he whisked on a black suit
And ran across the wall
And shouted, 'Matrix!'
And said, 'Wasn't that cool!'

Oh, the tales I could tell
And my dad's, well . . .
Passion to become a child.
However it would take page after page,
Up until now as we've
Locked him tight up in a metal bar cage!

Stephanie Clapp (11)
Kings Meadow Primary School

WHEN I SAW NIGHT

Night has no home and hardly anyone sees him,
His face is lonely, although no one has ever seen him,
When he talks his voices fades away.

Night cares for everyone and he protects them,
He makes everyone comfortable and sleepy,
His clothes are made from the moon
Which fade into his skin,
But yet he's lonely.

Adam Edmonds (10)
Kings Meadow Primary School

DEAR AUNTIE

Dear Auntie,
Oh! What a nice pair of trainers!
How clever of you to think of getting me
Pink Barbie ones.
They're so nice,
In fact they're so nice,
I think I'll keep them for best
And when I come to see you!
Thanks again!

Lauren Clough (11)
Kings Meadow Primary School

MY MUM'S FUNNIER THAN YOUR MUM

'My mum's funnier than your mum!'
'No, my mum's funnier than your mum!'
'Anyhow *my* mum's got a far smaller bum
Than your mum so there!'
'My mum is called Clair and your mum is called Fair so there!'

'Actually my mum changed her name to Meyer'
'Well, I don't think that's much better so there!'
'Well, I've got words to say to you and they are
My mum's still better than your mum so there!'

Alice Wise (9)
Kings Meadow Primary School

MY TRUE FRIEND

He's kind and nice, he will play all day
He'll play on the PS2 all the time with you
He's a nice bloke and he's loyal and not shy
He's clever, he's smart and he's very cool
He's got a funky name and my brother likes his hairdo
He wears a cap all the time, he's a natural too
He's funny and friendly, he's got a dazzling smile
And his name is
Kyle!

Jessica Martin (8)
Kings Meadow Primary School

SCHOOL

I hate school,
But my mum says it's cool!
I'm not too keen on the dinners,
Especially when it's fish fingers.
We sit on hard chairs,
In our uniform we wear flares.
At three o'clock, we go home,
That's my dream of the day!
When I'm home, I watch TV and *play!*

Shannon Walker (8)
Kings Meadow Primary School

THE SUN

As the sun goes down,
The tide slips away,
Beautiful treasures are left behind.

I see glistening, shiny sand,
Rocks covered in green, slippery seaweed,
Crabs peer up at me from their mottled shell.

Look through a glass window,
A magical, miniature world,
Starfish, anemones, urchins and shellfish
Are stranded until the tide returns.

Sarah Willacy (9)
Kings Meadow Primary School

PLUTO

Drifting through space
Lonely in his atmosphere
Wishing he was closer to other planets
Dust blowing on his surface
Icicles hanging from cave roofs
Shivering in the darkness.

Craig Whitty (11)
Kings Meadow Primary School

WIND

I am wind,
I arrive in a destructive tornado
I command you to wrap up warm
My bitter coldness
Blows a chill up your spine
I command animals to stay
In their burrows and dens
My gales blow roofs off houses
I wear a dark-black ghostly cloak
Which throws itself behind
And ruffles up around me
My whistling shout pierces your eardrums
I can make your eyes water
You cannot see me but I can see you!
I make the Earth crumble
With my awesome winds
If you try and light a fire, it will get blown out.

Michael Brindle (11)
Kings Meadow Primary School

WINTER

Very cold
Wearing woolly hats
We get well wrapped
We make snowmen and throw snowballs
Winter.

Ben Hopkins Hill (10)
Kings Meadow Primary School

MY PET, LOUIS

He has fur as black as the cloudy night,
Soft and smooth as I stroke him.
Eyes yellow and green as the feathers of a budgie.
He walks along silently,
His tail waving side to side.
He curls up in a ball like a hedgehog in his basket.

Jordan Wilson (8)
Kings Meadow Primary School

DAD

My dad, Trevor
Is very clever
He's got a hat with a feather
And he's got a coat and shoes made of leather
Which he wears when he picks the heather
He picks me up and says I'm as light as a feather
Don't you think my dad is very clever?

Laura Clarke (8)
Kings Meadow Primary School

COUSIN KATIE

My little cousin, Katie
Should be so really matey,
But she is so small
And I'm so tall,
I haven't seen her lately.
I know she's cute,
A little beaut,
My darling cousin, Katie.

Louise Slade (9)
Kings Meadow Primary School

A KENNING

A high pouncer,
A fast bouncer.

A fluffy ball,
A climbing the wall.

A mouse killer,
A milk spiller.

A clever walker,
A fast talker.

A catalogue to make me a *cat*.

Laura Howe (10)
Middle Barton Primary School

THE CAT

A playful friend,
A fluffy end.

A soft flop,
A ragged mop.

A dustbin hunter,
A home sleeper.

A catalogue to make me a *cat*.

Gemma Jackman (10)
Middle Barton Primary School

MY NIGHTMARE

A visible beast hides under your bed
Whilst dreams are skipping around in your head
It listens, it waits, it takes it all in
Ready to make you jump out of your skin

Its face is ugly with gloomy eyes
Above its head swarm lots of flies
Its breath is hot like boiling gravy
Its hair is short, dark and wavy

I start to sweat
I'm shaking too
It's getting closer
What do I do?

I hear a noise
Who can it be?
Someone, somewhere is calling me

The door swings open
Lets in the light
My nightmare is over
But it gave me a fright
For me that was a terrible night.

Lewis Fowler (10)
Middle Barton Primary School

FRIENDLY NIGHT

When every eye drops asleep
And the dream comes flowing through,
When the nocturnal animals come out to play
And the moon is their glowing eyes.
Every now and then a star will twinkle brightly
And a cold, brushy breeze comes swishing by.

People stop the noise which has gone on through the day
And we leave our troubles behind.
We remember the good things from our time,
The animals stay warm in their cosy, cuddly beds,
Everyone is sleepy with their head on their pillows
And that's how I think of night!

Marni Banks (11)
Middle Barton Primary School

LULLABY

Sleep, sleep tiny one, morning will soon be here,
You will then grow strong,
Tomorrow we rise bright and early,
So you and I will really see the world go by,
Sleep, sleep little one, it's time for you to sleep,
Tomorrow will bring fun and laughter,
Sleep, sleep, tomorrow will bring promises untold.

Timothy Clapham (8)
Newbottle & Charlton CE Primary School

AUTUMN

Tiptoeing along breaking branches
a tiny girl with fluttering wings,
her short, wispy hair floating while she flies,
her skin as white as snow.

Picking crispy leaves to make green trees bare
and painting silver frost over fish-filled ponds,
she blows her freezing breath to make it cold,
sprinkling autumn through the air.

Clare Hawes (9)
Newbottle & Charlton CE Primary School

SADNESS

Sadness is a forgotten grave
where nothing moves
and all is a dream,
like an undisturbed toy
lost under the bed.

Nick Swallow (11)
Newbottle & Charlton CE Primary School

SADNESS

Sadness is a fallen warrior
lying on the cold, damp earth.
He fought hard
and was left to die,
like meat-eater's prey,
cold and stiff.

Jonathan Stevens (10)
Newbottle & Charlton CE Primary School

GREED

Greed is the dark, blue sea
where it hits the rocks
and washes up the beach,
like the wind
at its kill point.

Emma Blake (11)
Newbottle & Charlton CE Primary School

SADNESS

Sadness is a lonely child
who's been tossed aside
by cruel playmates,
like a wild horse
exiled by its herd.

Sophie Jones (10)
Newbottle & Charlton CE Primary School

FEAR

Fear is a dark, black hole
that melts inside people's heads
while they are dreaming,
like a damp, dark subway
under a worn-out path.

Bethany Talbot (10)
Newbottle & Charlton CE Primary School

SADNESS

Sadness is a weepy funeral
that makes the church
dark and gloomy,
like a sad and bare prison
in unknown countryside.

Nial Hoggarth (10)
Newbottle & Charlton CE Primary School

MOUSE

Floorboard scurrier,
Morning time hurrier.

Cake taker,
Chocolate lover.

Night-time creeper,
Morning sleeper.

Secret eater,
Cat cheater.

Caitlin Joss (7)
Newbottle & Charlton CE Primary School

SADNESS

Sadness is an old dog
who waits in Heaven,
like an old tug boat
tied up in the harbour,
watching ships pass.

Tom Brown (10)
Newbottle & Charlton CE Primary School

SADNESS

Sadness is religious terrorism
where cranes dig for hopeful survivors
in dusty rubble,
like tiny creatures
searching for their food.

Emma Davidson (10)
Newbottle & Charlton CE Primary School

A FISHERMAN'S LULLABY

Sleep, sleep, tomorrow will bring shining fish,
Leaping high above flowing rivers.

Sleep, sleep, tomorrow will bring succulent salmon
Lying temptingly pink
On your plate.

Sleep, sleep, tomorrow will bring brown trout,
Camouflaged on the gravel riverbed.

Sleep, sleep, tomorrow will bring crunchy, battered fish,
Soaked in vinegar,
In its newspaper covering.

Ryan Knight (8)
Newbottle & Charlton CE Primary School

LULLABY

Sleep, sleep little one, tomorrow will bring
Delicate daisies budding in springtime.

Sleep, sleep little one, tomorrow will bring
Juicy hot dogs, dribbling with ketchup.

Sleep, sleep little one, tomorrow will bring
Happy holidays, family fun,
Walks along golden sands.

Sleep, sleep little one, tomorrow will bring peace to the world.
So sleep little baby, sleep.

Angelina Marsella Brookes (8)
Newbottle & Charlton CE Primary School

RUGBY DREAMING

Sleep, sleep my child, tomorrow will bring
Rugby tackling.

Sleep, sleep, players falling to the muddy ground,
Dirty and wet.

Sleep, sleep little one, tomorrow will bring
Exciting scrums, desperately heaving to win the ball.

Sleep, sleep, tomorrow will bring
A try scoring day!

Sleep, sleep little one, tomorrow will bring
The ball flying high between the posts.

Sleep, sleep, tomorrow will bring,
Bodies crashing over the line, again and again.

Sleep, sleep little one, dream of a win for your home team.

Daniel Welford (9)
Newbottle & Charlton CE Primary School

LULLABY

Sleep, sleep, tomorrow will bring
beautiful daisies with creamy petals.

The moon has come shining
like a milk chocolate button in a dark chocolate sky.

Sleep young one, tomorrow will bring
the postman on his rusty bicycle bringing exciting bundles.

Sleep, sleep, tomorrow will bring crisp white snow
like icing on a giant Christmas cake.

Cameron Anderson (7)
Newbottle & Charlton CE Primary School

LULLABY

Sleep, sleep little one, tomorrow will bring green bushes
blowing in the gentle breeze.

Sleep, await the warm sunshine
which will beat down on you.

Sleep, sleep little one, tomorrow will bring sticky marshmallows
melting in your mouth.

Sleep, sleep little one, tomorrow will bring golden promises
to your door.

Sleep, sleep little one, tomorrow will bring happiness
and hope for everyone.

Andrew Leith (8)
Newbottle & Charlton CE Primary School

LULLABY

Sleep, sleep little one, happy holidays are coming your way.

Sleep, tomorrow swimming through golden water,
past peaceful rainbowfish and crisp, white corals.

Sleep little one, tomorrow hot dogs galore!

Sleep, sleep little one, cup final wins for your special team.

Sleep, tomorrow will bring family fun,
playing tennis on the beach.

Sleep little one, tomorrow sailing into the future.

Carrick Barrons (8)
Newbottle & Charlton CE Primary School

MOUSE

Floorboard scuttler,
Night-time scurrier,
Naughty nibbler,
Cheese taker,
Noisy squeaker,
Messy eater,
Zigzag runner,
Tiny teaser,
Cat disliker,
Whisker twitcher,
Hole maker,
Cat's dinner!

Amelia Demicoli (9)
Newbottle & Charlton CE Primary School

AUTUMN

Climbing down a knotty oak tree
a young farm boy with conker skin.
Sack-made clothes dangling loosely,
leafy hair in torn straw hat.

Painting the sky with cloudy grey watercolour
and scaring migrators to warm skies.
He races the wind to make it blow faster,
singing autumn from his mouth.

Charlotte Oastler (10)
Newbottle & Charlton CE Primary School

THE CAT

Pitter-patter, tiny feet
Running quickly down the street
Purring loudly when he sees
That we have all come home for tea
Patiently he sits and waits
Until his food is on his plate
After tea he licks his fur
Then curls up cosily in a chair
Fast asleep, he sometimes snores
Twitches his whiskers, stretches his paws
When he wakes up, he washes again
Then he is ready to play a game
He chases a marble across the floor
When the game is over, he sits by the door
Out he goes to play with his friends
Until he wants to come home again
The cat is ours, we call him Jess,
We think he is the very best!

Daniel Altamura (8)
St Mary's CE Primary School, Banbury

A DOLPHIN POEM

A fish-eater
A bubble-user
A superb-jumper
A good-diver
A water-creature
A click-user
An excellent-swimmer.

Benjamin Wright (10)
St Mary's CE Primary School, Banbury

ALL SORTS

Some dogs are big
Some dogs are small
Some dogs are middle sized
But you can't have them all
You can give a dog a ball
But you won't make him sit for the first time at all

Dogs can be fluffy
When teaching tricks, it can be a toughie
After a day it can be enoughie

Well, you're hard at work
Well, in the house they like to lurk
A dog can be man's best friend
Even when you're off work, on the mend
But when you go on holiday, there's not a thing to lend
Dogs you cannot post, but photos you can send

Some dogs are posh
Some dogs are poor
But when they're hurt, they lie on the floor

If you don't play with them, their life will be a bore
When you feed them, they want more and more
If they're sad, try to make them glad
Because if you don't, they will behave bad
And if you don't, they will be worse and act mad

Dogs roll and make a mess
Even when you try to make them look their best
To be better than all the rest

Some dogs are big
Some dogs are small
Some dogs are middle sized
But you can't have them all.

Shelly Gibson (9)
St Mary's CE Primary School, Banbury

SCHOOL

St Mary's School is number one,
It's cool, it's great, it's really fun.
We have the best, the brainiest teachers,
Who work so hard to help and teach us.

In maths we are so very busy,
All those numbers make us dizzy.
We find those sums so hard to do,
Please be honest, didn't you?

History is so much harder,
Learning about the Armada.
Egyptians, Romans and Tudors,
All those dates, they do confuse us!

There is so much more we have to learn
And stars and certificates we have to earn.
We work and work with all our might,
We simply have to get it right.

There are many lessons we must know,
We must work hard before we grow.
When we succeed, it's really great,
So, learn it now, it's not too late!

Stephanie Timms (9)
St Mary's CE Primary School, Banbury

BEAUTIFUL SIGHTS

All the colours of the sunset,
Brighten up the night.
Red, orange, pink and yellow,
What a splendid sight.

All the bright stars in the sky,
Twinkle as they glow,
Way up high above you there,
It's like a little show.

Both the moon and shooting stars,
Are very, very high,
Looking down right over us,
From the big, black sky.

All these very pretty sights,
Are very good to see.
Every night, just look outside
And see paradise like me!

Kirsty Vincent (10)
St Mary's CE Primary School, Banbury

LIFE

Life is like a little stream flowing in the sun,
Life is like a river, meaning that it has only just begun,
Life is like the lake, so deep it's hard to get across,
Life is like the sea, so wild when you go over it,
You're not a child.

Leah Xandora (10)
St Mary's CE Primary School, Banbury

I LOVE YOU, MUSIC!

I love you, music,
You give me a right kick.
I listen to you in the car,
Even when I'm sick.

I listen to you all the time,
Before I go to bed.
You're taking over the world
And even in my head.

You come in tapes and CDs,
You're all over the shop.
I love you, music,
Classic, rock or pop!

Anna Faulkner (10)
St Mary's CE Primary School, Banbury

SUNFLOWER

I planted it in May
And it's grown today
Its leaves are dark green
It looks fun
And I'm glad it's done

It's brown in the middle
And it's yellow on the petals
It's the nicest one I've seen
I'm glad I did it in May
Because it's come out today.

Lauren Aisher (9)
St Mary's CE Primary School, Banbury

My Best Friend

My best friend likes a laugh,
Although sometimes she's pretty daft.
She mucks around most of the day,
Runs about and likes to play.

She's totally cool and lots of fun,
She's never nasty to anyone.
When I'm down, she's always there,
To put on my make-up and do my hair.

She stops over every week,
Makes Mum mad cos we won't sleep.
The reason why she's my best friend,
She's a groovy chick and that's the end.

Cassandra Fisher (11)
St Mary's CE Primary School, Banbury

Jacob . . .

Jacob's fur is silky and smooth,
He runs as fast as a tiger.
His body's shaved with a big bald patch
And his eyes are as brown as chocolate.
He has four handsome legs,
He's fit and strong
And he never goes wrong.
So watch yourself as he could back out,
Jacob's a gentle, fit pony!

Hannah MacLachlan (9)
St Mary's CE Primary School, Banbury

TREASURE ISLAND

A wonderful trip,
For *treasure!*
Load the ships,
All aboard!
Follow the map,
Enemies approaching!
Fire the cannons,
Yes!
The waves are getting fiercer now,
The captain said . . .
'I bet the treasure is full of diamonds and rubies.'
Golden sand,
Ringing ripples
And trees blowing in the wind.
Get into groups,
Get your shovels,
Look for treasure,
We've found it, with a note to say . . .
I hope you like the treasure.

Heather Trinder (8)
St Mary's CE Primary School, Banbury

POEM ABOUT PENGUINS!

Waddling across the freezing cold snow
With icy winds that like to blow
Waddling along in a pack so wide
Penguins freezing on the outside
Watching out for polar bears
Wolves and arctic foxes like to stare.

Annie Smith (10)
St Mary's CE Primary School, Banbury

THE KISS

The kiss made me blush and smile,
The kiss made me run a mile.

The kiss made me full of joy,
The kiss made me kiss another boy.

The kiss made me full of despair,
The kiss made me fall down the stair.

The kiss made me the happiest girl on Earth,
The kiss made me know what I'm worth.

Louise James (10)
St Mary's CE Primary School, Banbury

VALENTINE'S DAY

V alentine's Day is coming soon
A lot of love hearts everywhere
L overs buying beautiful flowers
E veryone getting soppy!
N o one fighting for a while
T ill Valentine's Day has gone
I n the night there's lots of kisses!
N ight-night
E veryone.

Emily Collison (9)
St Mary's CE Primary School, Banbury

SPELLS I

Boil trouble
Make it double
Newts' legs
And pink pegs

Old things
And harp pings
Clothes torn
And things worn
Fire logs
And lots of frogs
Make it fast
At half-past
Stars and sun
And a bit of fun
Rubbers
And scrubbers
Boil trouble
Make it double.

Emily Hartnoll (8)
St Mary's CE Primary School, Banbury

THE SEAL

A blubber body
A fat blob
A tail flicker
A fish killer
A night skiver
A scuba-diver
A quiet mouse.

Samantha Williams (9)
St Mary's CE Primary School, Banbury

A Spell Poem

Double pig's tail,
I don't want to fail,
Get me a dog
And a tongue of a frog,
Maybe some wool of bat,
Now what do you think of that?

Paul Corkish (8)
St Mary's CE Primary School, Banbury

Hidden Treasures

I step through the door into a mist of air,
I feel the warm breeze run through the ends of my hair,
I feel my lips starting to go dry,
My fingers start trembling through the blink of my eye,
I look ahead, there's a shining light,
I try not to look, as it's extremely bright.
My heart starts beating like the tick of a clock,
I start to wobble, but I try not to rock.
My imagination starts to spell excitement in my head,
There's a ringing bell inside me,
'Go on, do it,' the angel of me said.
I go into the room,
There's a chest I'd love to hold,
What's in it then . . .?
Wait there . . . it's *gold!*

Laura Bowne (10)
Southwold Primary School

GREAT WHITE SHARK

G reat, big, sharp teeth
R eally *dangerous*
E ats almost everything
A lways on the go for food
T eeth as big as your hand

W hy are we hunting them down?
H unters hunt them for fun
I t is quite enough, no more hunting them
T ime to stop those hunters
E at them for tea, don't eat me

S harks are cool, I mean it
H ave you got anything against them?
A re we going to help them or not?
R eally, they sometimes are nice and good
K eep them happy and you'll be happy.

Laura Dennis (10)
Southwold Primary School

SISTERS

M y sisters are so moody, they always get in a mood
Y ou are always telling them to be quiet

S tupid, silly and loud
I gnorant, fussy and not very nice
S elfish and horrible
T ease and taunt you
E verything they do bugs you
R eally wild and messy
S isters are a pest.

Natasha Burt (11)
Southwold Primary School

HIDDEN TREASURES

You're in a place where no one can see
Lonely, but you have me
With your long blonde hair and a heart of gold
No wonder you're a secret

You have a talent that no one else has
But why do you want to keep it a secret
Your voice is like an angel singing
It's in my head ringing and ringing

There's no one like you in the world
People say you are *fantastic!*
But when I look in your sparkling blue eye
I just realise you are a hidden treasure in my imagination.

Megan Duffin (10)
Southwold Primary School

HIDDEN FEELINGS

He was bottling up his feelings,
He was keeping them inside,
She was as precious as a china glass
And in no one could he confide.

Her hair flowed like a river,
Her features as delicate as can be,
He knew he could not win her love
And that thought was driving him crazy!

He was keeping his treasures hidden,
They were eating him up inside,
He knew he could not have her,
No matter how hard he tried.

Joe Chambers (10)
Southwold Primary School

GOLDEN TREASURE

You are very special and there aren't many like you;
You sparkle and you shimmer,
You are good-natured and kind-hearted.
You are charitable and generous,
You are so sweet and giving,
You share everything of yours,
Your eyes stand out with their twinkling yellow,
They glisten all around.
Below is your short, rounded nose;
Then your luminous gleaming teeth,
Which lay in your mouth with protection from your smooth, velvet lips.
You hair is short and sleek, covered in a rich, golden blonde,
It lies upon your rounded head with a layer of smooth, golden skin.
You live in a dreamt-of place,
Which is covered in velvety, golden sand,
That runs between your toes.
You are surrounded by palm trees, which are rough and have bristles.
But the sleek, glossy, emerald leaves brush against you.
Your home is an old, rusty, timber chest, with a colour of coffee;
It has blunt corners and is covered in fungus.
Although you glisten right out and make people happy
And you want to give people pleasure,
You only get a visit very rarely,
But you're strong and you won't fall apart.
You are wasted because you are hidden;
You deserve better, you are golden treasure!

Hannah Egan (10)
Southwold Primary School

GOLDEN DESTINY

Time goes by
And then you're seen.
He comes towards you,
Shocked,
Arms stretching out wide.
Every move he makes is seen
By your one empty eye.
Glistening and glamorous,
Not a speck of dust
Dares to land on you.
Onwards he creeps towards you,
Not believing that you're there . . .
There in the calm, dark, empty Mediterranean.
He speaks to you, asking if you're really there,
You say nothing,
Silence.
He grabs on to your clanking hand,
You don't move,
You're motionless.
Lifting you, arms aching,
Muscles straining at your heaviness.
Destiny that he sees
Is locked in
You.

Ciara Whitty (11)
Southwold Primary School

HIDDEN TREASURES

Hi hidden treasure, it is me.
You might not know me
But I have one question,
Where are you?
I know you are here,
Just show yourself,
Please come out,
It is your destiny,
You are evil now
I can feel it.
You take the life of people.
You are after me.
But tell me, what do you want?
My life and soul
Or me as your slave?

Ben Faulkner (11)
Southwold Primary School

HIDDEN TREASURES

A long time ago,
There was a ring,
A ring that was a piece of treasure,
A ring that was hidden,
Under the black sea,
The ring was gold,
It had strange writing over the sides,
It shone with glee,
Its diamonds sparkled to the sun,
But the ring was evil.

Daniel Finegan (11)
Southwold Primary School

Hidden Treasures

N   eighbourhoods, there's nothing like them
E   very place, peaceful and quiet
I   gnoring all the traffic and noise
G   entle drops of water falling from a pond in the garden
H   ear the birds singing tunes
B   eautiful flowers shimmer in the sunlight
O   range and yellow, the sun shines brightly
U   nderneath the beautiful oak tree
R   ipe apples sit on top of a tree
H   ouses sitting on the side of the road
O   n the top of the roof there is a cat
O   n the road there sits a colourful ball
D   o you want to live in a neighbourhood?

Becky Floyd (10)
Southwold Primary School

Treasure Day

T   omorrow is just another day
O   r should I say first of May
M   y summer is near
O   ver the pier
R   owing teams row in the summer sun
R   eady to have fun
O   r should I say I'm wrong, yeah
W   hat a surprise, what a *wonderful* day in May!

Gemma Green (11)
Southwold Primary School

HIDDEN TREASURES

You're like the sparkling sun in the bright blue sky
You are shiny and expensive
You make my eyes go blind
Your twinkling jewellery just flashes like the moon
You are in the old, dark attic with the mouldy smell
Far above my room
You live in the burgundy-red chest
You are beautiful and precious
Because you are the Crown Jewels.

Amy Harland (10)
Southwold Primary School

FORMULA ONE

F   ormula One racing teams
O   range overalls for Arrows
R   acing cars go round and round
M   otors extremely loud, zooming by
U   sing chequered flags at the end of the race
L   ap after lap after lap after lap
A   ctan, get ready the pet

O   ne and only Murray Walker
N   ew 3-seaters give thrilling rides
E   xtremely exciting and dangerous.

James Metcalf (10)
Southwold Primary School

HIDDEN TREASURE

Washed upon the sandy shore
A lot of people would think you're poor
In a rusty, brown, dusty and mouldy chest
Is the one and only diamond, plus the rest
I could go on forever
But I don't think you're worth it. Never

You never let anyone near
So everyone's full of fear
If you want to be spent
You better be prepared to pay rent
But I would be surprised if anyone came
Because you're all ancient and decaying, just the same.

Lauren Harris (11)
Southwold Primary School

HIDDEN TREASURES

Your hidden treasures get stronger
You can't doubt any longer
You try as you might but you don't know
Why you can't choose your feelings
Or your other side
So open your hidden treasures
To other people
And you might feel right
Or your hidden treasures will go
And your light
Will fade and float away.

Darren Millington (11)
Southwold Primary School

HIDDEN TREASURES

You have caused death, hatred and depression,
You thrive on betrayal, loneliness and war.
But yet you still manage to lure people in,
With your vibrant sandy-coloured home
And glittering contents.

Just answer me one question,
What do you want from me?
My soul and life
Or for me to be your eternal servant?

Joe Turner (11)
Southwold Primary School

I SAW . . .

I saw a peacock with its colourful tail,
I saw a blazing sun, rain and hail.
I saw clouds with flowers growing round,
I saw a spider creep on the floor.
I saw a rainbow swallowing a whale,
I saw a wet ship full of ale.
I saw water in the deep,
I saw an old man weep.
I saw the sun in night,
I saw the stars in daylight.
That is what I saw.

Kelly Phipps
Southwold Primary School

HIDDEN TREASURES

You were special to me,
Before you left,
Before you ran into the sun,
I know that that is your rightful home
You hatched at my feet
A baby, a child,
Mine.

Fire you once breathed,
I don't know where you are or whether you are still alive,
Nobody knew us together,
Your golden glow warmed me from the outside cold,
You were mine, a dragon.

Your egg I held in my arms,
I found you wrapped in seaweed and flames,
You give me hope, happiness, love, joy and magic!

Your hidden treasure is that you are the only one of your kind,
Heat filled my heart,
But,
It's cold now,
Come back to me,
My dragon child!

Aimi Keyser (11)
Southwold Primary School

HIDDEN TREASURES

I know you're hiding, somewhere here,
Surely you must be near.
It's getting late, I need to hurry,
But remember not to worry.
The clock's just struck, it's 12 o'clock,
There must be a key to the lock.

There's a shining light,
It's ever so, ever so bright.
The key fits the lock,
Dong! Goes the clock.
Yes! I say, I've found the gold,
It was exactly where I was told.

Zoe Smith (10)
Southwold Primary School

FORGOTTEN GOLD

Elevated on the top floor,
You're hiding from me.
In the piercing cold,
The attic, chalky, grimy and eerie.
Your many golden faces look around from the ancient chest,
Your home.

You're shy, you won't come out,
The dust tickles your cold, sleek body.
You are covered in dust,
But underneath you are precious, valuable and rule over all people.

You are envied by many
With your dazzling platinum looks.
You are pictured in a faraway place,
Where dreams come true.

You were loved as a child,
You lived in a different world.
Only now you are forgotten gold,
And you want it to stay that way.

Aimee Merry (10)
Southwold Primary School

SHE'S MY GRAN

She's hidden away,
Somewhere far away,
I wish I could see her every day,
But that is a wish that won't come true,
Unless I really believe in her.
I see her only once a year,
I go for Christmas and New Year,
She's always waiting there for me
And always has a surprise for me.
I wish I could see her every day,
Her face so pretty,
Hidden away.
She doesn't need make-up,
Just looks okay.
I hope she comes so very soon,
So there's someone to share my room.

Jennifer Young (10)
Southwold Primary School

HIDDEN TREASURES

Hidden treasures under the deep sand,
Spread all over your golden land.
But why are you sad,
When you are as rich as a prince?
And I have not seen you since
The first night you came to me in my dreams
And when I heard all of those screams.

What were you doing that night I ask?
Probably hiding all of your pearls, silver and gold,
Or we might have kept some.
You're no longer in my dreams,
You vanished
Only leaving some dust
And your gold in my dreams.

Jade Williams (11)
Southwold Primary School

HIDDEN TREASURE

You slowly walk
And seem to freeze time,
You stare,
You make me feel curious,
Your cold, icy presence
Is revealing a dark secret,
Shouting out a message,
You sometimes have anger
And hatred in your eyes,
Your long, white hair
Trails onto the floor,
You live in a photo,
Torn away
From my life . . .
Into another world.

Adam Verney (11)
Southwold Primary School

ENVIRONMENTS

E   veryone look at our environment
N   ever do we make it clean
V   ases full of flowers
I   nstead of our village green
R   un around on paving blocks
O   r on the grass in May
N   ever poison the air
M   ore of us will say
E   veryone is killing our environment
N   ow everyone stop
T   hink about what you're doing
S   top.

Rebecca Morgan (11)
Southwold Primary School

TREASURE

T   reasure that Blind Pew loves
R   obbers and his crew love it too
E   meralds and diamonds
A   nger and greed
S   hips sail full of gold
U   nderground caves with treasure chests
R   ead the map and find the gems
E   veryone dreams of being rich.

Rupert Taylor-Allkins (10)
Southwold Primary School

THE DOLPHINS

T he dolphins swim under the moon,
H ave smooth skin like velvet,
E veryone comes to see and doesn't hesitate.

D own under the water is where they live,
O ceans calm as they leap,
L ovely animals they are,
P laying around under the midnight breeze.
H appy mammals as they sing,
I n the oceans and seas is where they have been seen,
N othing can change the way they are,
S tars sparkling under their eyes.

Olivia White (10)
Southwold Primary School

TREASURE

T reassure shining in the light, hey, look at the glitter sight
R eal, golden, shining like the stars
E verywhere they are glittering in the sky
A t moonlight the treasures come out to play
S ounds of glitter that sound like waves
U p in the sky glittering so high
R eal, living, attractive treasure
E verybody's looking at the beautiful things of living treasure.

Rachel Palmer (10)
Southwold Primary School